Building Total Enterprise Asset Management Solutions

A Guide to Capital Needs Analysis

By
Douglas K. Christensen
Cameron R. Christensen

Building Total Enterprise Asset Management Solutions:
A Guide to Capital Needs Analysis
www.BuildingTEAMSBook.com

Copyright © 2018 Cameron R. Christensen

All Editions

Graphics and images contained herein are used with express permissions from APPA: Leadership and Educational Facilities.

Graphics and images contained herein are used with express permissions from Dana K. Smith, FAIA, DKS Information Consulting, LLC

Editor: Edit My English
Cover Design and Book Format: Lori Christensen

Table of Contents

Dedicated to a visionary man who believed
Facilities Management was all about building relationships.
My mentor, colleague, friend, hero, and father.

Acknowledgements

Thank you to all who made this journey possible and supported the visionary development of Capital Needs Analysis and Total Cost of Ownership.

Thank you to APPA and the Center for Facilities Research who supported the effort, sponsored research initiatives, and provided a forum where these principles could be cultivated into an industry-wide paradigm shift.

Thank you to the editors, readers, formatter, graphic designer, and all who have been instrumental in making this book a reality.

Author Acknowledgements

Douglas K. Christensen

I appreciate the support of my family members, especially the support and love shown by my parents, Mr. and Mrs. Keith W. Christensen, who have always been excited and supportive in the pursuit of worthwhile goals.

I express my love to my children, Caryn, Coray Douglas, Camille, and Cameron Ray for their patience and love during this endeavor.

I express my sincere thanks and love to my devoted wife, Linda, who sacrificed the time needed to complete this research effort. Her devotion and support truly made this research effort possible.

Cameron R. Christensen

I appreciate the numerous colleagues and mentors who supported and encouraged this project and contributed to the paradigm shift that embraced these principles.

I express my heartfelt love and appreciation to my family for their encouragement and unwavering support of this goal.

I express my sincere love and appreciation to my dedicated wife and best friend, Lori, for her patience and support during this effort. Without her talents, this book would not have been realized.

About the Authors
Douglas K. Christensen

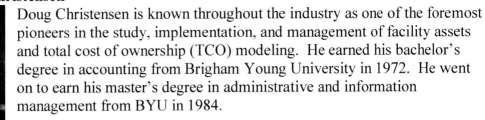

Doug Christensen is known throughout the industry as one of the foremost pioneers in the study, implementation, and management of facility assets and total cost of ownership (TCO) modeling. He earned his bachelor's degree in accounting from Brigham Young University in 1972. He went on to earn his master's degree in administrative and information management from BYU in 1984.

After working as the Business Manager for Auxiliary Services and Director of Physical Plant, in 1980, he was asked to take on a temporary assignment for the university. The charge came directly from the board of directors to complete an assessment of the campus needs for the next ten years. While engaged in that effort, he led the development of a revolutionary method for planning long-term needs on an ongoing basis without the need for costly periodic condition assessments. In 1989 he was offered to head the newly established Capital Needs Analysis Center for the university. The next 31 years, spent in the study, implementation, and management of facility assets and total cost of ownership modeling, contributed to a world-wide paradigm shift in the facilities management industry.

Christensen has authored numerous peer-reviewed articles and given dozens of presentations on the subject. In 1987, he was awarded the Rex Dillow Award from APPA: Leadership in Educational Facilities for his article titled *Integrating Capital Studies within Physical Plant Operations*. In 2004, the BYU Capital Needs Analysis Center was the recipient of the APPA Effective and Innovative Practices award. Also in 2004, he was among the first to receive the designation of APPA Fellow.

Christensen always felt that knowledge should be shared. In addition to his publications and presentations, he was dean of the APPA Leadership Academy and taught Asset Management for the BYU Facilities Management program. He hosted seminars and workshops educating facilities professionals on the principles of effective asset management. In 2016, he was asked by APPA to be one of three steering committee members to lead the development of a standard for the American National Standards Institute on total cost of ownership modeling.

For years, it was his desire to codify his life's work into a book that could be shared throughout the industry. In August, 2016, he was taken from us too early, before he could finish and publish his work. This book has been produced as a culmination of his research and writing efforts.

Cameron R. Christensen

Cameron Christensen started his career in the built environment working as a landscaping laborer in 1996. He was soon promoted to foreman and trained as an irrigation specialist. With that experience, he secured a position as an entry-level HVAC technician on the campus of Brigham Young University while he pursued his bachelor's degree. Those early experiences working in the field "turning wrenches" were an important part of the foundation laid for his development as a facilities professional.

Christensen was awarded a bachelor's of science degree in facilities management from Brigham Young University. While a student, he completed internships with the Physical Plant and the Capital Needs Analysis Center, learning about capital needs planning best practices. He also completed an internship where he conducted facility condition assessments for Asset Evolution. Since completing his undergraduate degree, he has worked in project management, operations management, and senior administration in facilities operations from coast to coast. Above all, his greatest experience was learning from his mentor and father, Doug Christensen.

Christensen has continued his education throughout his career. He earned an MBA in finance from Walden University as well as a master's in real estate management from New England College. He has pursued numerous professional certifications and credentials including APPA's Certified Educational Facilities Professional, IFMA's Facilities Management Professional, LEED Green Associate through the US Green Building Council, and Certified Building Operator from the Northwest Energy Efficiency Council.

Christensen is an active member of APPA. He served on the committee for part one of the APPA-led effort to develop an American National Standard for total cost of ownership modeling. He currently sits on the committee to develop part two of the standard focusing on implementation of TCO.

Foreword
By E. Lander Medlin

This body of work is not only a tribute to the facilities management profession but to its creator, Doug Christensen, and its faithful translator, Cameron Christensen – his son. Promises made in life are difficult to keep in death, but Cameron indeed kept his promise to publish the culmination of his father's work, this seminal manuscript *"Building TEAM Solutions"*.

I knew Doug, like many of my fellow colleagues, as a mentor, sage advisor, colleague and friend. This book takes me back to so many treasured conversations. As the philosophies and principles, processes and practices for the management and leadership of the facilities profession unfold throughout the book, I am sure those of you who knew Doug will hear his voice come through loud and clear. For those of you meeting Doug's work for the first time, buckle up, it's going to be a transformational ride! Doug was a visionary, principle-centered, mental giant. Certainly ahead of his day in espousing such timeless principles. He also knew full well that people are at the heart of it all stating, *"Facilities Management is People Management; we bring the buildings along for laughs."* From beginning to end, this asset management program thrives on collaboration.

We are living in a world where the speed of change and the speed of learning is at the speed of now. Becoming continuous learners was something Doug knew way early on as captured in a quote from the *Wrap-Up section*: *"Recapitalization is the learning organization of facilities managers . . . recapitalization management, using life-cycle and total cost of ownership principles, is a platform for change."*

As you can readily surmise, I highly recommend this book as a must-read not only for those new to the field of educational facilities management, but for those seasoned professionals to get grounded in the principles and practices of total enterprise asset management.

About this Text

In 1984, as part of his master's thesis titled *A Study of Decision Criteria for Major Replacements, Renewals, and Planned Improvements at Selected University Campuses*, a young Doug Christensen wrote the following:

> Today, procedures are being suggested as to how to determine what the real needs and priorities are for a university. In the future, these suggested procedures, and the resulting information, will assist administrators in determining what needs are important and how they assist in forming more specific priorities. However, the main concerns seem to suggest that confidence and understanding as to what is a priority, and how it is determined to be a priority will be the important questions...
>
> Due to the increased importance of knowing how to manage aging facilities on university priorities, an exploration is needed to determine present decision patterns by physical facility administrators (physical plant).[1]

These words were nothing short of visionary. At a time when long-range facility planning was in its infancy, Doug Christensen wrote about the need to be more forward thinking and strategic in the administration of physical facilities. From his first asset analysis in 1972 until his death in 2016, Christensen devoted his life's work to the study of strategic facilities planning. Starting with life-cycle projections of the Capital Needs Analysis Center at Brigham Young University and throughout numerous presentations, seminars, journal articles, and interviews, he was a champion and collaborator at the forefront of the development of total cost of ownership modeling of physical facilities.

This text is a compilation of the collaboration, research findings, and best practices that Doug Christensen employed in his work. It will delve into the strategic foundation of long-range facilities planning and the need for leadership in those efforts. It will outline methods for organizing the effort and determining the best means and methods to establish and operate an enterprise asset management solution. Lastly, this will touch upon the role of life-cycle planning in the overall total cost of ownership model.

Throughout his life, Christensen felt that knowledge should be shared. He espoused the notion that "a rising tide raises all ships." By sharing all that he learned, he felt he was doing his part to grow the industry toward a more strategic method of leadership.

In addition to his seminars and published articles, it was his intent to author a text to be used to share this knowledge of how building Total Enterprise Asset Management or *TEAM* Solutions could impact the strategic plan of organizations. This text constitutes the portion of his research and writings that are specifically centered on effective capital needs planning as an investment strategy. While he did not live to see this work published, it does contain the introduction he wrote for the text, excerpts he wrote both for this text and other works, as well as many of the research findings and illustrations he developed both in an individual effort as well as a collaborative product with other colleagues. This text is aimed at sharing his findings and to help future generations benefit from his life's work.

---

[1] Christensen, *A Study of Decision Criteria for Major Replacements, Renewals, and Planned Improvements at Selected University Campuses.*

Author's Note by Cameron R. Christensen

When I was a young student at Brigham Young University, I struggled with the decision on which field of study to pursue. I had been admitted to the university under a music scholarship intending to study performance and music education. However, I quickly learned in that first year, while although this was a passion, it was not what I wanted to do for a career. While evaluating my options, I turned to my father, Doug Christensen, for advice. He suggested that I sit down with Jeff Campbell, the chair of the Facilities Management program at BYU and see what it was about.

When I met with Dr. Campbell, I was thrilled with what I learned. I had always been partial to the built environment but the Facilities Management program brought the elements together in such a way that I was intrigued at the possibility of a career in the field. When I discussed this with my father, he explained his perspective and thoughts that it was a fit match for my interests. Until this point, I knew he worked for the BYU Physical Plant (whatever that was) but didn't really understand what he did for the university.

It wasn't until my first APPA Annual Meeting in 2003 that I began to understand what he meant to the industry and the impact that he had made throughout his career. By this time, I had completed an internship with the BYU Physical Plant and spent some time with the Capital Needs Analysis (CNA) center. I had developed a strong interest in the principles of CNA and the impact that effective long-range capital planning would have on the success of an institution.

While in a breakout session of the conference, the moderator presented several case studies, and we separated into groups to discuss and comment on them. By chance, the case study assigned to my group provided the profile of a large religious institution with approximately 30,000 students, approximately 10 million square feet, facilities used seven days per week, doubling as centers of worship for the student body on weekends and, among other things, no backlog of deferred maintenance.

As I listened to my table-mates discuss this profile, their key takeaway was that the capital study must be a mistake. "No campus has zero deferred maintenance" was their conclusion, and their recommendation was that the capital study be redone because it was obviously inaccurate. I indicated that I believed it was possible but the opinions of this student did little to sway these seasoned professionals.

As someone from our table explained the conclusion and recommendation, the moderator patiently listened to their reasons and then asked the full group if there were any other thoughts on the matter. There were several agreements from other tables that this study was clearly incorrect. The moderator simply said, "Interesting. Thank you for sharing these thoughts. Let me introduce you to the only man that I know who has zero deferred maintenance. Doug Christensen, come up here and tell us how you did it."

For the next several minutes, I watched in awe as my father captivated the audience in describing the BYU CNA process and the success that they had enjoyed since the center's founding. Before that time, I had no clue just how great of an accomplishment his life's work had been and what it meant to so many other campus operations. That experience sparked a passion in me to follow his lead and learn as much as I could about those principles and apply them however possible.

Many have tried to adopt the BYU model and met with success. When I describe the BYU model to colleagues, I frequently hear "It won't work" or "If we had the resources of BYU, we could do that too." When I explain to them that this process has been adopted at other organizations ranging from large universities to small nonprofits, minds become opened to the possibility.

When my father became ill, I made my best efforts to be with him as much as I could. During my visits, we would talk about many things, but he would always seem to light up and have more energy whenever the topic came around to CNA or total cost of ownership. At the time, he was on the steering committee for the APPA-led effort to develop a TCO standard. Since he couldn't participate in the ways in which he was accustomed, he wanted frequent updates and would ask questions to make sure we were "doing it right." He was still committed to the development of the standard and the furthering of these principles.

In July, 2016, I visited him in the care center for what I felt would be the last time. His health was on a steady decline, and there was little else that could be done to reverse the trend. When I walked into the room, he greeted me by saying, "Hey! I'm glad you're here! We have a lot of work to do!" I looked at him quizzically and responded, "What do you mean?" He said, "I want to talk about you finishing my book." At first, I objected—indicating that I couldn't possibly measure up. He assured me in his gentle, confident way that I could handle it and that this was something he wanted to ensure was completed.

We then spent much of the next three days talking about what to include in the book, as well as the outline and format. While he hadn't done much of the writing, he had done some, and told me that I could find it on his computer back at the house. I recovered the electronic files along with boxes full of papers, including reports, drafts, charts, and old PowerPoint presentations he had developed. I began reading everything he had written on the subject preparing to pursue the last professional request he had asked of me.

As I started writing, I often felt his influence throughout this project. I would stop frequently and think, "Is this what Dad would say?" and not rest until I felt confident it agreed with his teachings, writings, and overall philosophy.

For this text, I have three hopes. First, it is my hope that, for those reading this who knew him, they will once again hear his patient, gentle, wise counsel and remember him as the industry giant we all knew. Second, for those who did not know him, it is my hope that you will gain an understanding of the tip of the iceberg that was his life's work. Lastly, it is my sincere hope that you will find something of worth in this book to adopt into your operation contributing to raising the tide of the industry, thereby lifting all our collective ships to the next level.

Introduction by Douglas K. Christensen

Since the beginning of my professional work in 1972, there has been a lot of change surrounding the facilities profession—a maturing process. Being an accountant by schooling and later gaining a master's of administrative and information management, I found myself right in the middle of the transformation. Adapting these learned skills to the facility management profession has been the joy of my life, and I can truly say there has not been a single challenge or opportunity that has not come my way.

Drivers

The profession of Facilities Management has continually shifted and different drivers of change have had their influence on the field.

Societal Change

Moving from an industrial-driven society to an information-driven society has been an ongoing challenge. Facilities, unlike people, stay put and either blend in with the adjustments or are pronounced unusable. Adapting to the pace of ever-changing demands in an information age has put stress on existing investments and existing resources to care for assets. The decision points on where to continue to invest, with limited resources, has questioned the knowledge and wisdom of the times. Better decision making has become a requirement for the facilities manager and prioritizing essential needs has become the curse of the facility leader.

Technological Change

The move to the information age first started as an impact on existing investments in buildings and infrastructure, and then progressed to the enhancement of the profession. The buildings that were designed in the 60s, 70s, and 80s were intended to provide different learning and teaching environments. The methods of educating shifted from a lecture presentation, strictly in the classroom, to where we are today with the whole world at the fingertips of students and professors. In addition, the learning environment has changed from a "teach me what you know" system, to self-learning, where the teacher is the facilitator of knowledge.

This new method requires a different kind of environment where what is learned may require different assets to search for answers. How professors and students communicate within new environments takes a reinvestment in existing assets. This new paradigm greatly affects the physical learning environment. The wonders of technology have quickly become the reality. The use of equipment requires additional utilities to operate and cool the space. This surprise impact caused a significant demand on resources. The cost of retrofitting the learning environment to accommodate these demands almost doubled because of the expense of adding technological equipment.

Resource providers have accepted that technology is not going away and that it continually changes. The challenge was, and still is: How do leaders make good decisions given limited resources? Which resources are critical? How do you get a handle on the impact technology has had on existing and new space design and construction?

Economical Change

The last forty years have seen an up and down economy. The education industry progressed considerably during most of these years because it continued to grow and invest. The growth of campuses, buildings, and new systems increased needs. Very little was done to balance this growth with sustainable resources. New construction allowed for a lot of this development without the consequences of resource shortages. In the 2000s many new buildings opened without operating resources, which added greater concern for the overall health of the education industry.

Investigations and research into the "why" has revealed that the decision makers used limited funds and made decisions on how to best invest in expansion assets. This caused an imbalance of resource needs. The focus was on the noise of the moment and not on the critical resources that would insure the institution's ability to meet its long-term mission objectives. Competition for students added pressure to the mix and tuitions were rising faster than inflation. The economy stopped producing jobs, so funding for students and families was tight and job-seekers during those down times rushed to get schooling. However, poor investments in the existing campuses made it hard for some institutions to compete in the new expanded student market. Decision makers were asking questions about how and where limited dollars should be invested. What are the critical issues when resources become tight and what level of funding is needed?

Resource Change

Resource change covers a lot of areas. Funding from sponsoring providers such as legislators, churches, and private funding were scattered. The issues of limited resources grew over the 40-year period.

The fully funded, well-endowed institutions were not short on capital funding. However, those that were lacking in financial backing created a term called "deferred maintenance," later called "deferred capital renewal." This was the lack of funds needed to keep the institution going. The point was that institutions did not have resources to maintain the level of current investments and the pressures of adding new technology needed to keep up with the trending changes in education required resources they didn't have. The buildings and infrastructures were ignored unless there was failure. The demands of maintaining old buildings meant key structures crumbled and needs for emergency care expanded. Regulatory and compliance issues were approved, but most were unfunded mandates, crippling their ability to see the projects through to completion. These issues piled on to the capital funding needs. This also affected the operating budgets. More repairs were financed from operating funds, thus reducing the care and operations of working assets.

As the industry changed from a fund accounting concept to a Financial Accounting Standards Board (FASB) and Government Accounting Standards Board (GASB) method of accounting. These accounting practices caused institutions, for the first time, to recognize that the resources needed to be whole. Like a business, this new accounting reporting format gave leadership a better picture of what the resource needs were for existing investments. But implementing the full picture seemed impossible to most.

Here is the reality of it. There will be fewer institutions in the future because of these strains as most of them are resource poor. Leaders and managers will need data and information so they can use the knowledge to be proactive with future resource needs. Resources for capital assets will always be limited. Finding ways to manage those assets so the greater need is met will be integral to the decisions of future leaders. Without clear, data-rich resolve, there is very little hope that the resource levels required will be met so that administrators and investment leaders can be sure that their continued investment will meet the most important needs of the institution. Leaders will need to find ways to make sure that "*expectations + needs = the resources available.*"

Changing of the Guard

Another critical resource need stems from the vast turnover of qualified workers and leaders. The workers of today are not as well trained in the skills needed to manage a campus. This shortage in skilled labor will provide additional opportunities for leaders to deal with it properly. The concern is that even if the resource levels are improved, who will be skilled enough to hire?

With every challenge comes an opportunity. The current facilities leadership will soon be retiring. What a great challenge it will be to live in the existing world with existing resources and processes. However, beyond that hurdle is a greater prospect for the profession: to introduce new, proven, and focused ways of doing business with different tools and processes.

Taking advantage of this dilemma will require leadership. Leadership action is choosing what is best for the future. How does the current situation deal with the needs of the future? Those individuals who hire facilities leadership need to be aware of the opportunities that exist to change for the better. Hiring of replacement personnel needs to be based on the ability to deal with the current situation as well as challenge it.

The stewardship role of the institution's existing capital investments is the largest role at the institution. Knowing the mission and vision of the institution and where it is in relationship to that future is critical to its success and the life blood of the institution. Determining how the complete facilities organization can support and stand behind the right change is important.

Very few leaders would tackle the future without some commitment to dealing with expectations. These must be clear and there needs to be a corresponding effort on all sides to see this to a better end. Identifying the best path to follow establishing metrics to measure progress is an important step. The challenge of the future will be to see how facility and educational leaders decide to deal with the management of existing investments, given limited resources and an environment that continues to change. One solution is to accept the "new." New approaches can result in better solutions. This book is all about having a successful future and becoming heroes to the institution—its vision and mission.

Technology in the Profession

The last great evolution over the past 40 years has been the introduction of technology. The amazing ways in which varied people and occupations have gone digital has revolutionized the way we communicate and conduct business. I remember when the first PC was introduced. Our department had a reason to talk via a computer with financial services but we still did not trust the outcome. I remember spending hours verifying that what went over the wires was correct. I even bought one of the first "portable" Compaq computers. It had a small screen and weighed a ton. It was not very portable.

In 1980, I was asked to computerize the Physical Plant. At the time, I thought we were the last holdout. A lot of other departments had computers and had gained expertise in using them. We had none. In fact, I was asked to do this right after the previous director had retired. I asked Sam Brewster, the retiring director, why it had taken so long to get into technology. With a smile he said, "They were not going to do any computers while I was the director." Since nothing had been done, a clean set of objectives lie ahead.

The main driver, at first, was to bill the customers and then send the data to Financial Services, and thus, the learning curve began. Our profession has not effectively used technology to increase the productivity even today. This delay is due to the stubborn nature of not choosing to find a better way to do business. As technology has improved and influenced most all professions, the path to helpful technology is at the front door.

Many facility organizations computerized existing business processes without taking full advantage of the paybacks of technology. Only now are great productivity savings being realized in facilities management procedures.

How can decision makers improve the bottom line of all owners? How can newer technology deal with limited resources? How can professional facility managers be of greater value to the profession? Where do the savings come from?

<u>Focus</u>

Learning and applying answers to these valuable lessons over the past 40 years has given me a very good picture of the future. It involves three focus areas that are common concerns to most owners:
1. Resource planning
2. Project delivery
3. Life-cycle maintenance

We learned that a focus on capital assets is key to discovering the right systems for the future. Managing the capital investment life and its value to its mission and vision allows facility managers the opportunity to take that investment and manage its potential. Learning to do this focuses on the key principle that managing the capital assets life-cycle is the best way to maximize the investment.

The greatest returns in assets, systems, and components are to maximize the investment life. The companion to this understanding is the practice of asset life-cycle maintenance. This book is based on what was learned about managing assets through their life-cycle in the context of total cost of ownership. Methods have been developed to build better decision making around asset investments. These decisions include the "birth and burial" investment costs, "maintenance and operation" investment costs, and "recapitalization" investment costs. Once owners know what the investment cost decisions are, they and their investors are then able to measure the return on that investment.

Simplicity

It is possible to make complexity simple:
> *Simplicity is the Ultimate Sophistication.*
> ~ Leonardo da Vinci

Our goal is to have a very sophisticated approach to simplify capital needs analysis.
> *Making the simple complicated is commonplace;*
> *making the complicated simple, awesomely simple, that's creativity.*
> ~ Charles Mingus

This approach to capital needs planning will be awesomely simple and very creative.
> *Sometimes the questions are complicated and the answers are simple.*
> ~ Dr. Seuss

Management and investors are very complicated in the way they question the resources they invest.
> *Genius is the ability to reduce the complicated to the simple.*
> ~ C.W. Cream

The genius of bringing best practices to the industry will provide a solution that is simple and powerful. There is not enough time to have complicated results.
> *Ability is what you're capable of doing.*
> *Motivation determines what you do.*
> *Attitude determines how well you do it.*
> ~ Lou Holtz

Hopefully, the years of experience transferred to the readers and users of this book will motivate them to find better ways to run their operations. The future will require a different attitude and some strong inspiration to get it done.

> *Life is really simple, but we insist on making it complicated.*
> ~ Confucius

This is our gift to the hardest working profession – simple solutions to complex issues.

This book is designed to take the complicated nature of this profession and find simplicity. Put the wisdom of good decision making back in the hands of those who care for the asset investments (see Figure i.1).

Determine the **data** needed and turn that into **information** that serves a purpose. That purpose should lead to **knowledge** of what is happening. Knowing what is happening at all steps of an asset's life gives the decision maker a focus on when to take additional action. As knowledge is gained and experience is applied, there becomes an **understanding** of the value of the invested asset and the possibility of additional

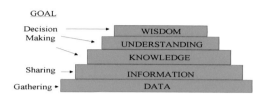

Figure i.1
Data Maturity Model

investments if needed to extend its useful life. This understanding will help decision makers share in the reasoning that goes into making **wise decisions** for those who invest. This is all about helping decision makers make correct decisions through a simplified set of data.

Enjoy the learning. Enjoy the journey.

Douglas K. Christensen

Part I: Foundation

Chapter 1: Understanding Total Cost of Ownership

"Total cost of ownership asset management, where all costs are being tracked, requires work but will save money."
~Douglas K. Christensen[1]

Introducing Total Cost of Ownership (TCO)

The concept of total cost of ownership (TCO) is not new and the principles have been acknowledged throughout history. As economies, governments, technology, and social drivers change with time, the facilities management profession must also adapt to the shifting environment. For a profession that was once predominantly reactive—waiting around for the phone to ring—the need to have greater understanding of the built environment has led to such innovative changes as the incorporation of preventive maintenance, building automation, life-cycle planning, computerized maintenance management, computer-aided facilities management, building information modeling, geographic information systems, and a multitude of micro and macro paradigm shifts that have driven these evolutions. They all have their place in the industry and effectively maintain their stewardship of the built environment. However, if not managed properly, silos can exist that prevent effective means of integrating the most valuable offerings of each contributor (see Figure 1.1).[2]

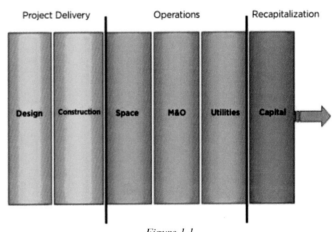

Figure 1.1
TCO Management Silos

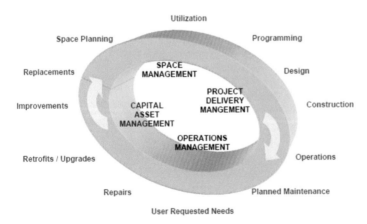

Figure 1.2
Asset Life-cycle Model for
Total Cost of Ownership Management

In its simplest terms, TCO seeks to break down those silos. According to APPA's Center for Facilities Research (CFaR), "TCO includes the total present value of all direct, indirect, reoccurring, and non-reoccurring costs incurred or estimated to be incurred in the design, development, production, operations, maintenance, and renewal of a facility, structure, or asset over its anticipated life span."[3] It is a concept that seeks to unify competencies managed by different functional groups to ensure that physical assets are designed, constructed, maintained, and renewed as a holistic strategy with the goal of maximizing the return on investment for the owner (see Figure 1.2).[4] The basis of the TCO principle is that each asset expense needs to be managed and leveraged against the limited resources available. Maximizing the useful life of the asset investment is a "best in class" practice.

In order to understand how TCO can maximize the investment strategy of an institution, one must first understand all the costs of the model and how they integrate with each other.

TCO Framework

The total cost of ownership framework has three primary cost groups: birth and burial, maintenance and operations, and recapitalization (see Figure 1.3).[5] Within each of those cost groups are the primary cost classifications related to the management of the costs of physical assets.

Birth and Burial

These costs are also identified as non-recurring costs as they only occur once in an asset's life. This group is a frequent builder of silos. Often the approach to design and construction, either by coincidence or design, encourages isolationism from the other functional groups within the built environment. Some have overcome this challenge and coordinate well with other groups, while others have not. Abundant opportunities to maximize return on investment and minimize total cost of ownership reside in this stage of the TCO framework. There are a multitude of philosophies across the full spectrum of possibilities on how to integrate the cost groups and break down these silos in order to draw out the full potential of these opportunities.

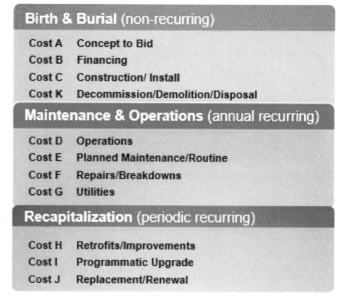

Figure 1.3
Total Cost of Ownership Framework

To ensure that facilities are designed and constructed in a maintainable way, the maintenance organization of the institution must be engaged from the conceptual start of the project. Too many times, the maintenance group is brought into the picture to review final construction drawings ready for or already out for bid. Oftentimes, they only get one or two walkthroughs during construction as a courtesy and informative process but not as collaboration on the end product. They are brought in during the final phases of commissioning, after which there are often required adjustments to sequences of operations, equipment, and overall function of the assets. Involving maintenance operations early on as a partner and full stakeholder in the process, rather than as an interested end-user, will help identify opportunities to develop a more efficient design, construct a more maintainable facility, and maximize return on investment.

Painstaking efforts are frequently undertaken to reduce the cost of planning, design, and especially construction activities. Terms like "value engineering" have become commonplace in the industry vernacular and are accepted as synonymous with cost cutting. However, emerging research has suggested that only 33% of a facility's total cost of ownership is in birth and burial activities.[6] The remaining costs, 67% or more of a facility's total costs, are in subsequent cost groups that take place after commissioning and occupancy. A modest investment during construction, if done right and in a data driven manner, can result in a lower overall total cost of ownership and greater return on investment. Hence, this is why it is vital that the planning, design, and construction group integrates fully with the maintenance and operations group.

Maintenance and Operations
Maintenance and operations constitutes the largest of the three cost groups. These are the annual, reoccurring costs that are used for preventive/predictive maintenance, repairs, utilities, and other operating activities of the asset. It is in this group that there is typically the greatest opportunity to maximize return on investment. Conversely, if managed poorly, it has the greatest potential to produce unnecessary costs for the organization driving up TCO through increased utility costs, breakdowns, more frequent repairs, and other failures due to a lack of proper maintenance.

One key element of maintenance and operations with the integration into the TCO framework is ensuring effective data management. This topic of how to effectively manage data will be discussed in greater detail in other sections of the text. The more data that can be made available related to the specific asset, the more information management will have on how best to ensure that the maximum return on investment will be achieved. Better data leads to better design decisions when the time comes to renovate or construct. Better data will provide more perspective on historic asset costs and identify best practices and applications for assets and asset classes when recapitalization decisions come about. As stated previously, data is the foundation that will lead to the understanding necessary to make wise decisions.

In *Birth and Burial*, potential silos leading to obstacles in information-sharing were identified. Those same obstacles exist in *Maintenance and Operations*. If asked, technicians will have no shortage of new and creative imageries they employ to refer to their opinions of what was designed and constructed. Yet, many are reluctant or unable to provide useable information that could help inform and improve those designs. Since they lack readily available data, they provide anecdotes and historical information which may or may not be applicable or relevant to the asset-centric discussion at hand. In a world where this data is readily available, these anecdotes can turn into data-filled discussions that lead to better designs by the architects and engineers, more maintainable finished products, greater cohesion between the two groups, and overall lower total cost of maintenance.

Maintenance departments are in an exceptional position to collect great amounts of data. They can use it to make wise decisions on how frequently to do preventive maintenance, when to cycle equipment to avoid peak energy demand charges, which repairs would be worth the cost, and which assets are becoming more costly to retain. However, if that data is never shared with the planning, design, and construction group, they cannot incorporate that experience into the development of new facilities. Ensuring systematic reporting or some data transparency mechanism will start to break down information silos that will provide the ability to make wise decisions leading to the design and construction of more maintainable facilities.

Recapitalization

Recapitalization management is the focal point of this text. While great care must be taken to managing the birth, burial, operations, and maintenance costs, it is when the asset comes due for recapitalization that the most intensive decisions are made about reinvestment. It is during the discussions on recapitalization that all the data related to design, construction, operations, maintenance, utilities, and other elements that have been collected over the life of the asset take center stage. By utilizing that historical data, when it comes time to recapitalize the asset at the end of its life-cycle, that data can be put to use to make wise investment decisions and compound the impact by potentially lowering the overall total cost of the other two cost groups as well.

To start with the end in mind, there are three decision points at which an asset will be considered "end of life." It is important that managers have each of these in mind when maintaining assets. The longest possible life-cycle is not always the lowest overall total cost of ownership. Many times, replacing an asset before it fails may be more cost effective.[7] There are three types of life-cycles that are introduced below and addressed in greater detail in Chapter 8.

> **End of Investment Life-cycle.** This is when the determination is made that it is more costly to keep the asset in operation than to replace it.[8]
> **End of Useful Life.** Useful life is considered spent when "the usefulness of the asset does not meet the mission or future vision of the owner."[9]
> **End of Life-cycle.** When an asset starts to enter a period where permanent failure is imminent or has already occurred, the asset is considered at the end of its life-cycle.[10]

TCO and Strategic Asset Investment

The primary aim of TCO is to maximize the return on investment of the physical assets of the organization. This is accomplished by establishing a vision by which all other components and sub-components of the model are managed. It establishes a series of questions and criteria that provide achievable benchmarks and place the data in more manageable extents without neglecting the bigger picture.

One of the more visual tools developed to help ask these questions is the Strategic Investment Pyramid (see Figure 1.4).[11] The Strategic Investment Pyramid was developed by APPA's Center for Facilities Research to identify critical decision factors relative to effective asset investment strategies. More details can be found in the APPA Center for Facilities Research publication, *Buildings... The Gifts that Keep on Taking*. This section is intended to provide a brief overview and present this as an assessment tool that can be used throughout this exercise.

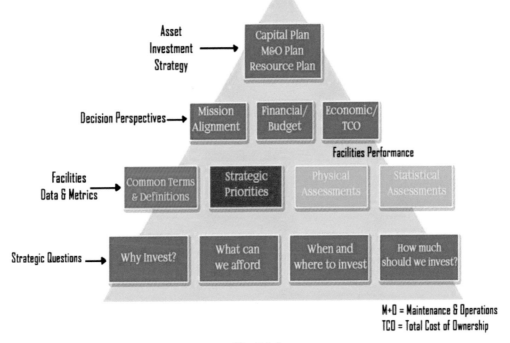

Figure 1.4
Strategic Investment Pyramid

Foundation: Strategic Questions
As with any investment strategy, this integrated decision framework is built upon a foundation of strategic questions. Those foundational questions are:

- Why invest?
- What can we afford?
- When and where should we invest?
- How much should we invest?

These are questions that should be asked and used as the guiding vision for the purpose of investing. They help to ensure that limited resources are not being wasted.

Metrics and Indicators
Now that the Why, What, When, Where, and How of the strategy has been established, it is essential that these questions are answered using data and comparative metrics. Without data, strategic questions remain philosophical and cannot be quantified nor compared.

To have a common understanding of the statistical data, a common vocabulary must be utilized. There are many standards and documents that help professionals gain an understanding of terminology commonly used throughout the industry. As an example, professionals in the industry frequently refer to a unit of measure as square footage. However, when utilizing comparative metrics, it is important to know which square footage calculation is being referred to. Gross square foot? Net square foot? Assignable square foot? Rentable square foot? Cleanable square foot? Maintainable square foot? Only by first ensuring a common unit of measure and a means of calculating that unit of measure can an apples-to-apples comparison be possible.[12]

Because resources are limited, prioritization must be done. This is best accomplished by developing an objective matrix whereby various needs can be scored and ranked. This matrix needs to be adopted by all, especially the senior leadership in the organization; otherwise, executive priorities risk jeopardizing the capital plan. Whatever that prioritization strategy is, it must be rooted in the organizational mission and ratified by the senior leadership, or it has a high probability of getting derailed. This topic will also be addressed in greater detail in Chapter 5.

Terminology and prioritization remain only as conceptual tools without the data to back it up. The Strategic Investment Pyramid refers to two types of data assessments. The first is physical data collection through periodic assessments. This is captured by taking a physical inventory of the assets and completing visual, non-destructive, destructive, ultrasonic, thermal, and other types of testing and analyses aimed at ascertaining the current condition. This approach has a high potential for accuracy, as a technician is visually ascertaining the data. While there is always opportunity for error, the ability to physically inspect these assets provides an advantage.

While a physical inspection may provide a greater degree of accuracy, it is also very time consuming, and the data can be arduous to manage. This is especially true in smaller operations where the administrative support may not be as abundant. In these situations, incorporating some degree of statistical analysis into the formula may help to ease those burdens. The second type of data assessment, statistical assessment, uses an algorithm of formulaic computations to ascertain the expected life of the asset based on a number of variables. This assessment is different for each asset classification, and manufacturers and consultants can help with developing these formulas. More details will be provided regarding data gathering in Chapter 5.

By using a combination of physical and statistical assessments, the goal of developing life-cycle projection data for capital needs planning may be in reach regardless of the size of the operation and the availability of resources to manage the data. The objective for each operation is to strike the right balance of physical vs. statistical assessments. Some organizations only conduct physical assessments of major assets, such as central heating, cooling, and roofs; while smaller units and systems, such as air handlers, pumps, split systems, electrical distribution, and plumbing systems are evaluated on a statistical basis. Others have the resources to inventory a greater share of the assets and only rely on statistical assessment for larger building systems where physical inventory is not feasible.

It is important to consider the long-term implications of this balance. While there may be abundant resources now to collect the data, using consultants as an example, what will be the resource availability down the road for managing it? Many enterprise asset management programs fail because they find that management of the data is too cumbersome and they abandon the effort. Ensuring that the process and data is at a manageable level within the resources available is a key to long-term success.

Decision Perspectives

Once data has been gathered and analyzed, decisions start to be made about what is to be done. Prioritization matrices should be established to help streamline decision making. However, even with prioritization matrices, chances are, there will not be sufficient resources to go around. This is where effective decision making plays a vital role in the Strategic Investment Pyramid.

There are three elements to effective decision making when allocating scarce resources. All three should be considered together equally, and the needs that best fit all three criteria should receive top consideration.

Mission Alignment. Mission alignment of capital needs principles is vital when making recapitalization decisions. Without a clear understanding of the mission and objectives that the asset is serving, useful life decisions cannot be made. Implementation of an asset comprehensive plan (see Figure 1.5) is an important step in being able to ascertain an asset's useful life.[13]

An asset comprehensive plan incorporates the capital needs, operations, and growth of the organization into the total cost of ownership strategy. Without maintaining each of these outlooks, the separate initiatives have a tendency to become siloed and less efficient. As a result, the overall cost of the built environment begins to climb. Bringing these areas into harmony under one strategy will begin to set the stage for an effective total cost of ownership perspective.

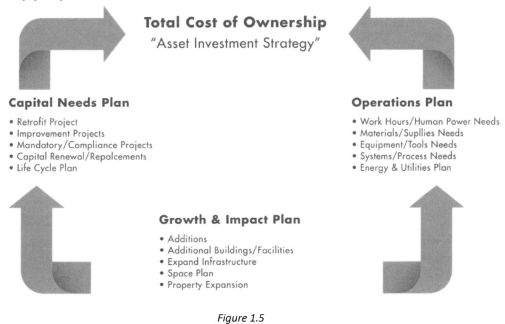

Total Cost of Ownership
"Asset Investment Strategy"

Capital Needs Plan
- Retrofit Project
- Improvement Projects
- Mandatory/Compliance Projects
- Capital Renewal/Repalcements
- Life Cycle Plan

Operations Plan
- Work Hours/Human Power Needs
- Materials/Supllies Needs
- Equipment/Tools Needs
- Systems/Process Needs
- Energy & Utilities Plan

Growth & Impact Plan
- Additions
- Additional Buildings/Facilities
- Expand Infrastructure
- Space Plan
- Property Expansion

Figure 1.5
Asset Comprehensive Plan

Ensuring that resources are allocated to needs that are aligned to support the mission is key to success. If a mission fit cannot be found, resources should not be allocated; it's that simple. Pressures arise from customers, executives, politicians, and the community—all valuable stakeholders and individuals that need to have a positive relationship with the organization. Being able to "tell truth to power" in these circumstances can be challenging. Having these tough conversations without damaging relationships takes tact and diplomacy, but they need to be had in order to ensure that resources are being directed to initiatives that are going to support and advance the mission of the organization.

Having clear mission dependency matrices and prioritization strategies documented and ratified by the senior leadership of the organization will help to provide a foundation on which to build. In many of these conversations, the requestor will not need to be told "no" and explained why. Simply sitting down with the requestor and having a frank conversation with regard to mission dependence and prioritization may prompt him/her to recognize that the initiative may not be supporting the mission in the way it was envisioned. What may also result is an amended initiative that is more of a mission fit and can be supported and pursued as such.

All that being said, not every project request is going to fit like a perfect puzzle piece into the strategic plan. Some are going to be more impactful than others. Each project, need, and initiative is different and should be handled as such. There is no magic formula or outline. The key is to keep focused on the mission and safeguard the resources for pursuit of those objectives.

Budget and Financial Resources. Even the most strategic, mission-aligned asset management plan must have the financial resources to support it. Including the financial management offices of the organization in the conversation will help to ascertain the available funding opportunities. Not all funding opportunities need to be internal, budget-allocated funds. There are other opportunities such as grants, loans, bonding, performance contracting, state appropriations, and other vehicles that can be used to support the capital plan. Depending on if the organization is public, private, or nonprofit, resources may be within reach that have gone untapped. Reaching out to peer organizations, colleagues, and professional associations can help to develop a fairly comprehensive list of the options available.

Once these funding options are known, it is essential to pair each initiative with the most fitting vehicle. For example, while replacing a chiller may be possible with internally allocated funds, there may be energy efficiency programs that will partially or fully fund the replacement. For any project with a potential energy payback (HVAC equipment, roofs, windows, etc.), it is recommended to package the project as an energy conservation measure to determine the attractiveness to energy grants, performance contracts, and financing opportunities. Finding these alternative sources of funding will free up internally allocated resources to address the more routine maintenance efforts that would be more challenging to fund externally.

Economic and Total Cost of Ownership. As emphasized in *Buildings... The Gifts that Keep on Taking*, "Total cost of ownership is, by far, the most overlooked element in the decision-making process for investing in facilities; yet it is a fundamental cornerstone of the Strategic Investment Pyramid."[14] It is by understanding and employing the total cost of ownership model that decisions can be made that will maximize return on investment. This text is not intended to be a comprehensive discussion on the modeling and practice of TCO.

Rather it is a detailed guide to establishing an effective capital needs program to manage the recapitalization of assets at the end of life. Because TCO is such an integral part of capital needs planning, it will continue to be referenced and discussed at great length throughout the text.

Chapter 2: Leadership, Change, and Strategy

*"I am responsible for this but I've got to change how we do business
and take that responsibility and go to the next level and
find what the direction is."*
~Douglas K. Christensen [15]

During an interview by APPA in 1995, Doug Christensen defined leadership in this way:

> *Leadership is three basic things: One is it defines a direction, a vision of where you want to go. Second is it really talks about aligning constituencies. How do you get people and systems and structures to align with where you're going? And the last is, how do you motivate and get enough energy to get to the next level or direction you're going?* [16]

Before implementation of any of the TCO principles can be attempted, questions need to be asked about leadership and change management strategies. In his book, *On Becoming a Leader*, Warren Bennis reminded us, "It is not enough for a leader to do things right; he must do the right thing."[17] This frequently articulated mantra is oftentimes not fully understood. Common sense dictates that if an operation is considering implementing a capital needs analysis strategy, it is not currently managing assets in a manner that is satisfactory and, therefore, needs to change the way it does business. In short, the organization must feel the need to "do the right thing." This chapter will identify foundational elements on shaping the question, "What is the right thing?"

Leadership and effectively implementing change strategies are essential components to any long-term capital needs planning system. Change requires leadership. There are entire libraries, bookstores, and online databases that could be filled and overfilled with all that has been written about leadership and change management. Rather than attempt to present a "new idea" when it comes to leading change initiatives, this text will highlight some of the best practices required when implementing asset-centric management and address how those concepts play a role in the success of the initiative.

There are many theories on the most effective way to pursue a change management strategy. From John Kotter and his penguins to Motorola's principles of Six Sigma, there are dozens of "leading theories" on managing change and quality initiatives. Through most of these concepts, there are some consistent best practices that frequently make an appearance.

Sense of Urgency / Define the Problem

Before a vision can be set and before we can have the end in mind, we must identify where we are and the nature of the problem. As of 2007, it was estimated that nationwide there was a cumulative backlog of deferred capital renewal among higher education institutions exceeding $36 billion.[18] Many facilities professionals attribute this growing problem, and rightly so, to a reduction in allocated resources by administrators and legislative appropriators.

"...there are a lot of people confused by it. If they're looking at it as a management issue, then all they look at is a reduction in resources, and we just don't know what we're doing or where we're going. If they look at it as leadership, they're saying, 'Oh, I am responsible for this but I've got to change how we do business and take that responsibility and go to the next level and find what the direction is.'"[19]

In *Buildings... The Gifts that Keep on Taking*, the authors recognized that there has been a reduction of resources contributing to the problem of a growing backlog of deferred capital renewal.[20] As they suggested, and the ten years since the book's publication have verified, the trend is not going to reverse. This reduction of resources, doing more with less, is the "new normal."

Although resources are shrinking, the physical portfolio is not. Conversely, new facilities are oftentimes constructed with little to no thought to long-range planning of maintenance, operations, or recapitalization. These actions, while seemingly short-sighted, are often the result of a lack of information in the project delivery phases of TCO. Keeping a total cost of ownership mindset will inform the design selections and help to maximize the return on investment while offering a perspective on what should be funded for maintenance, operations, and recapitalization. Having those discussions 10, 20, or 30 years after occupancy when assets begin to reach the end of their life makes it challenging to have any meaningful impact on the investment of the facilities portfolio.

However, better late than never. For existing buildings, developing a case for an investment strategy can be a "Catch 22." On the one hand, the new system would be playing catchup from any number of years of operation without a long-term recapitalization strategy. The backlog of deferred capital renewal can be expensive to clear. On the other hand, selling the program conceptually may be easier to do with realized quantified data rather than theoretical projections.

Ask any facilities professional about their facilities and most can rattle off the top of their heads current or upcoming critical capital needs that require action, but few have an articulated life-cycle plan. They may have an old facility condition assessment sitting on the shelf, but the data might be out-of-date and needs to be refreshed. Herein lies the dilemma for many: how to create a sense of urgency and articulate the problem to senior administrators with little or no data and few resources to obtain the data.

Like the old proverb says, "A journey of a thousand miles begins with a first step." Establishing a sense of urgency of the problem at hand is the keystone of the change process. Without an understanding of the appropriate gravity of the situation, administrators and appropriators will not appreciate the data and the impact of inaction. While this text will offer some suggestions, there are dozens of possible ways to approach shaping this argument. Means and methods should be tailored to meet the needs of the audience for maximum persuasive impact.

Most operations have rudimentary sets of data already in circulation, while some have a wealth of data at their disposal. Helpful data could include work orders, labor hours, actual expenditures, overtime costs, maintenance logs, breakdown or repair histories, lists of equipment needing to be replaced, customer or staff climate surveys, or any number of data points that could help to illustrate the point.

It is important to assess what data resources are presently available and how they can be tailored in order to convey the message in a way which best communicates the urgency to the audience that receives it. If it is the CFO, for example, highly technical information may not be effective. The data should be centered on financial impact and return on investment, the information that s/he will be primarily concerned. If it is the provost, dean, or academic affairs committee of an academic institution, an illustration of the negative impact these conditions or systems failures have on the learning environment may be the most appropriate. Highlighting what this information means for the stakeholder receiving the information will have a more meaningful effect than a one-size-fits-all report.

Lastly, the information must be supported and realistic. While doom and gloom predictions may get some hearts pumping, they are less convincing than plausible scenarios that have a foundation in supported fact. Savvy leaders can find creative ways to use the data available to paint an appropriate picture of what is needed and the consequences of inaction. Without the use of solid data and realistic scenarios, the gravity of the situation may not be appreciated or the audience may not fully understand the challenges.

Set the Vision / Begin with the End in Mind
Once urgency is established behind a shared concern for the problem at hand, a team of stakeholders can collaborate to establish a vision of how the capital needs planning process should function. At this juncture, it is essential to assemble the team of stakeholders who will have ownership of the process and collaborate to ensure the program is well-rounded and has the ability to achieve its full potential. It is vital to have a clear vision of what is wanted regarding the outputs of the program and build it from there.

At this point, no data has been gathered; no analysis has been completed. Yet, establishment of a vision for the future is possible. Baseline analytics give us a starting point and certainly help shape the journey. However, vision is based on completely different criteria.

Setting the vision of the program begins with the strategic mission of the overall organization. Whether that is a college or university, governmental facilities, corporate real estate, or manufacturing, the vision of that organization must be at the heart of the effort. Setting a capital plan or master plan contrary to that strategy would be counterproductive and a waste of resources.

Once the vision is determined, it should be articulated in written form. A clear and concise statement of the intent and desired objectives of the effort will help to serve as a beacon throughout the process and ensure that all facets are evaluated and developed in a holistic manner.

Collaborate on Strategy
Once the vision is set, the next step is to develop the plan to achieve it. For a long-range capital plan, it is entirely possible that the vision will be a fluid, moving target and never be

fully achieved. The strategic plan to achieve the vision should be flexible enough to adapt to the shifting priorities of the organization, changes in organizational strategy, as well as in the executive leadership that will impact the capital planning process.

Several exceptional industry tools can help to shape a strategic plan. Whether formal analytical systems are used, such as Balanced Scorecard, The Baldrige Framework, Six Sigma, SWOT Analysis, or a home-grown method, it is important to have a framework to follow.

In order to garner a full appreciation of the multi-faceted needs of the program, multiple stakeholders from a variety of functional areas throughout the organization need to be included in the team. This team is key to the long-term success of the program. It cannot be just engineers and facilities professionals. There must also be a boots-on-the-ground presence from front-line technical staff. The **technical** team, consisting of facilities professionals and the front-line technicians, will ensure that the program considers maintainable solutions as well as building codes, regulatory requirements, and industry-specific trends. There also needs to be an advocate for the **financial** and procurement requirements of the organization. A **customer** advocate is necessary to ensure that the end user needs and the external customer experience are safeguarded. Lastly, there must be an advocate for the executive **strategy,** ensuring that the program goals do not conflict with the overall direction of the organization. Only at the intersection where demands are being considered and balanced will the full potential of the capital planning process thrive (see Figure 2.1).

Figure 2.1
Strategic Balanced Demands

With all that taken into consideration, it is important that the final program does not degrade into a camel (a horse built by committee). The effort requires strong leadership with an understanding of the needs and a vision of the organization. Without a strong, savvy leader at the helm to wrangle in digressions as well as prompt ideas and productive debate, the true potential of the effort could be jeopardized resulting in a watered-down, overly bureaucratic shadow of what was intended. ***Leadership is everything***.

Set and Achieve Milestones
Now that the vision and strategy have been set, the team must set a path forward. The details of each effort will vary from operation to operation, but the basic skeletal structure should be the same. The text goes into greater details in later chapters, but key milestones that should be included in development and implementation of the program include:

Setup

Organization

- ✓ Organize the new enterprise asset management program to ensure mission alignment
- ✓ Establish guiding principles for the program
- ✓ Establish key roles of individuals that will maintain the program
- ✓ Determine assessment level or levels to be pursued

Inventory and Initial Projections

- ✓ Establish a location hierarchy
- ✓ Identify assets or asset classifications that will be included in the program
- ✓ Identify a classification standard, whether that be in-house developed or an industry adopted standard (i.e., OmniClass, Uniformat II, ASTM FACTS, etc.)
- ✓ Establish asset naming conventions and nomenclature
- ✓ Establish asset prioritization strategy
- ✓ Identify the primary system of record to store and manage the data
- ✓ Inventory all managed assets
- ✓ Compile initial reporting and projections
- ✓ Project annual funding needs

Establish Program Quality Assurance

- ✓ Establish standards and develop a standard operating procedures guide
- ✓ Conduct training of all personnel that will play a part in the program
- ✓ Develop means to audit and confirm data and activities that are completed according to the standards established

Administration

Zero Tour Condition Assessment and Decision Making

- ✓ Conduct the first "Zero Tour" condition assessment of all assets with "zero" remaining life
- ✓ Evaluate the results of the Zero Tour and make decisions
- ✓ Prioritize projects to be completed
- ✓ Evaluate funding opportunities

Reporting and Execution

- ✓ Report to senior administration or executive team
- ✓ Execute project delivery plan
- ✓ Execute continued management
- ✓ Audit database and data

Maintain the New Program

Now that the strategic goals and objectives have been determined, it is vital that the new culture be shaped to survive the ever-changing environment. The rate of technological development is constantly yielding new ideas and new demands on the built environment. As technology changes, the industry progresses and customer demands evolve. Organizational strategy must shift in response. The new asset management initiative will be fragile. In order to ensure that it will be able to survive in a shifting environment, periodic review and adjustment must be built into the standard operating procedures. Without periodically reviewing the program and adjusting to meet changing demands, any shift from the norm could be seen as requiring a change initiative rather than a simple correction of the program as already strategized.

Chapter 3: Articulating the Business Case

"The goal for any business ought to be to create a culture where decisions are made using knowledge and understanding."
~Douglas K. Christensen

Throughout the capital needs planning process, the end goal of the program must always be kept in mind. The ultimate objective of asset management and life-cycle planning is to support maximizing the return on physical facilities investment of the organization. As aptly articulated in *Buildings… The Gifts that Keep on Taking*, the author indicated:

> *Application of a business case analysis to any investment in facilities is important, because an institution's decision makers should always consider scenarios in which the mission can be achieved within incurring the expense that comes from facilities. Building more space should never be the sole option.*[21]

Many times, organizations seek to build their way out of a challenge with the built environment rather than evaluate all the available options. As illustrated in Chapter 1, total cost of construction is only about one-third the total cost of ownership. By constructing a new building rather than evaluating other possibilities, the organization may be creating more fiscal challenges in years to come rather than strategically addressing the issue at hand.

There are several aspects of the effort to maximize return on investment that need to be continually considered. Much has already been said on integrating principles of total cost of ownership modeling, as well as maintaining a mission-driven focus. Another key factor in this effort is continually articulating the business case.

Articulating the business case is not a one-time presentation held with senior officers of the organization to share the idea of capital needs planning. Many facilities leaders have had this meeting and thought they were done, only to find out months or years later that the message didn't sink in or resonate the way they had hoped. Articulating the business case is a continual conversation incorporating those concepts into every facet of the long-range planning effort. It will take a kickoff meeting and dozens of other formal and informal encounters to engrain the concepts into the organization.

Know Your Audience

Arguably, the most critical aspect of articulating the business case is knowing the audience. Knowing and speaking to the audience simply ensures that the aspects of the capital needs process that most closely align with their goals and objectives are clearly communicated. Even the most conclusive data is ineffective if it cannot be conveyed in such a way as to allow the receiver to understand it, care about it, and utilize it in the intended way. Discussing delta-T and sequences of operations may be fine in the central plant working with the chief engineer, but when engaging with the CFO, more attention needs to be paid to project cost, justifications, objectives, customer impact, and return on investment.

In some organizations, getting to know the audience can be quite a simple process, since they are colleagues who frequently interact with many levels of the organization. They have a great deal of access and transparency that allow the staff to understand what matters to them and how best to articulate concerns. In other organizations, there may be a shroud of uncertainty and mystery with the senior leadership. This may stem from a desire for privacy or just simply because their portfolio is too large to entertain a more individual approach to the way they do business. Regardless of the reason, understanding how they process information and what they care about is key to success.

The Need for Accurate Data

A strong business case begins with compelling, accurate data. Exaggerations and inflated projections may provide short-term gains but are not long-term strategies that ensure sustained support of the initiative. Eventually, the inconsistencies with correct performance indicators will reveal the discrepancies and all assumptions, projections, and conclusions will be called into question. Trust is a difficult thing to gain, especially after it has been tainted by controversy.

Accurate data can be gathered from a number of sources. For the full picture to be captured, data elements from all aspects of the total cost of ownership model should be taken into account.

Project Delivery

For project costs, data can be pulled from historic projects of a similar size and scope. Networking with other operations of a similar size, mission, and duty can be excellent sources of costing information. Professional consultants, architects, and engineers, while on the more expensive side, can provide estimates of the project costs. Also, there are costing systems like Whitestone© and RS Means© that provide regional averages of costs either by asset or assembly.

Operations and Maintenance

For operations and maintenance data, metrics and manufacturer guidelines do exist to help with forecasting the cost of O&M activities. However, each operation is unique and the most accurate data will come from the activities of the team doing the work. Work orders, daily time sheets, preventive maintenance logs, repair histories, and other sources of information are helpful in ascertaining the true cost of activities.

These data points are best summarized so each building, system, and asset can be dissected in order to understand the true total cost. Without having this granularity, understanding the cost and reliability of certain assets is much more challenging and far less certain. Managing at the building level will be helpful in understanding which building on campus requires the most attention. However, the asset manager will not be able to understand which asset or system is creating those demands without those additional levels of detail. Having that fine granularity will drive asset replacement decisions and help ensure that life-cycle data is correctly assessed and forecast.

It is important for each operation to decide how detailed the record of these activities should be. The more granular the data available, the more valuable it can be in ascertaining where the most impactful opportunities are. On the other hand, the more detailed the data, the more effort required to maintain it; hence, the importance of finding the right level of granularity for the operation that provides the requisite value without being overly burdensome.

Energy and Utilities
A key data point in understanding the total cost of an asset and determining if a similar asset or something different should be forecast for replacement is the energy consumption data. There are many ways to capture this data. One of the more effective ways is sub-metering the large equipment such as chillers, boilers, air handlers, rooftop and AC units. Building sub-metering, while not as effective, can also answer questions of total cost and identify opportunities for reducing energy consumption through equipment replacement and renewal. Lastly, and the most cumbersome, is estimated runtime logs from the maintenance team. This is costly, time-consuming, and has limits with regard to its accuracy. With the reduced costs of sub-metering systems, data loggers, and the availability of funding opportunities for these activities, very few justifications remain for operations to not move in this direction.

Whatever the method used, getting the most accurate data possible on energy consumption is an important piece of the puzzle when assessing if an asset should be deferred, renewed, or replaced. Without this metric, an assessment of investment life-cycle cannot be completed.

Recapitalization
Even before the new capital planning system has generated years' worth of data, there is likely still data that can be gathered on recapitalization and renewal. Gathering all the information possible from various sources on when assets were installed, replaced, overhauled, or retrofit will help to build an initial life-cycle database that will establish baseline life-cycles for the current equipment. This will assist in providing more accurate projections.

As the capital planning system continues to operate, the life-cycle data will become increasingly accurate for the unique conditions of their environment and duty. Ensuring as many data points as possible are part of the system, such as installation date, current replacement value, life-cycle, manufacturer, model, serial number, size, energy consumption, runtime, repairs, preventive maintenance, and failure rates will provide sufficient context to make wise recapitalization decisions and ensure informed asset selection at the time of replacement.

Foundation of Data
While accurate data is essential in building a competent business case, it is important to remember the role of data in decision making as well. As illustrated in the Data Maturity Model (see Figure i.1), data is the foundation of wise decision making. In 2006, Thomas Davenport wrote in the *Harvard Business Review,* "Employees hired for their expertise with numbers or trained to recognize their importance are armed with the best evidence and the best quantitative tools. As a result, they make the best decisions."[22]

This is no less true while planning for the capital needs of an organization. Data from areas of project delivery, operations, maintenance, utilities, and recapitalization are essential in order to make decisions that would maximize return on investment and lower overall total cost of ownership.

Persistence

The final principle of articulating the business case is persistence. When the concept of capital needs planning at BYU was first theorized, it was started as a part-time experiment to see what would come from looking at their assets in this way. It did not start out as a paradigm-shifting initiative. It was a simple idea that developed through persistence. After years of data and proving the value of the decisions born out of that data, the university ultimately established the CNA Center.

The first data set and capital needs reports may not convince many. There may be several on board with the concept of the plan who are enthusiastic in the beginning. However, when times get tough and they look to reduce resources, if they are not convinced of the value the program is providing, capital projects are easy targets for budget cuts. It is important to not lose sight of the end goal and the potential that the program can provide. By patiently persisting and proving that the program is adding value to the organization, resistance to regressing to a lesser program will be supported.

The Cost of Inaction

There is an old saying that there are two types of people in the world, "those that earn interest and those that pay interest." Likewise, there are two types of facilities professionals; those that plan for failures and those that don't. Granted, not every failure can be planned for, but the more that can be anticipated through life-cycle forecasting, inspection, and condition assessment, the more it will save the organization on the cost for the emergency repairs.

There is an old saying in baseball coined by Tommy Lasorda: "No matter how good you are, you're going to lose one-third of your games. No matter how bad you are, you're going to win one-third of your games. It's the other third that makes the difference." The same is true in the facilities profession. Every facility has assets that are functioning and will continue to do so with proper preventive maintenance. Likewise, every facility has assets that fail before their expected life-cycle even with proper maintenance. So it follows, by implementing a proactive maintenance and asset management program, assets that may have otherwise failed will continue to operate and add value to the organization.

Just as baseball teams enter each game not knowing the outcome, facilities professionals also need to address the maintenance and planning efforts of assets to ensure that those "games" that can be "won" have the best possible outcome. This requires a comprehensive strategy on developing standards that can be supported across the board. Without implementing proper maintenance and asset management practices, those "games" that otherwise could have been "won" will be lost, and the unexpected cost of replacing assets in an emergency will diminish the organization's overall ability to reinvest in their capital infrastructure.

Standards

The first critical step in assessing the cost of inaction is to establish standards. A framework for establishing standards in the context of an enterprise asset management program will be discussed in Chapter 6. For this context, it is important to understand the role of standards and the cost of compromising on those standards when it comes to the business case of the new initiative.

Standards need to be established with the total impact of failure in mind. Fiscal prudence and the opportunity cost of cash reserves for asset replacements is important and should always be weighed. However, it is also important to consider other influences that are not just economical. Factors that may also be considered when establishing standards include damage to reputation, loss of business, decreased ability to raise funds, and lack of investor and trustee confidence, among others.

Once established, those standards must be adhered to. In the event that a particular standard cannot be met, the questions should be asked, "Do we have the right standard for this asset or system?" or "Should we re-evaluate our standard for this asset or system?" It is important to return to the four foundational questions in the Strategic Investment Pyramid (see Figure 1.4):

- Why invest?
- What can we afford?
- When and where should we invest?
- How much should we invest?

Compromising standards is a slippery slope. There is always an argument for something that appears to be more important at the time. Having a well-run, well-maintained facility can lead decision makers into a false sense of security. It is tempting to pull resources from asset management activities when failures are few and far between. However, by doing so, the organization is setting itself up to turn the tables and find out what is on the other side of that fence.

Cost of Emergencies

Depending on the project, an emergency replacement can cost as much as three to nine times the cost of a planned replacement. Each asset or system is different and will have different impacts. Table 3.1 provides some examples of how proactive, planned replacement can be superior to waiting for the asset to be in imminent risk of failure (or already failed) before planning for replacement. This is not intended to be a comprehensive list but rather to illustrate potential opportunities and impacts.

	Table 3.1	
	Possible Opportunities Associated with Planned Replacement	**Possible Impacts Associated with Emergency Replacement**
Asset Failure	Delivery before failure and loss of business	Unexpected loss of business or occupancy Create a hazardous condition
Mission Fit	Ability to analyze the asset mission fit and future plans	A type-for-type replacement regardless of needs or future planning
Planning & Analytics	Engineering of replacement asset based on current and future needs	Rushed engineering and analytics if completed
Evaluation of Options	Evaluation of various options and comparison of total cost of ownership impact	Comparison of total cost of ownership likely omitted in the name of expedience
Bidding & Procurement	Bid process ensuring a competitive price	Abbreviated bidding process compromising competition
Project Delivery	Strategic project delivery allowing for the most cost effective and least disruptive means and methods	Rushed shipping and fabrication costs Expedited project delivery requiring rework Greater likelihood of unforeseeable conditions

Spending to Save

As the old saying goes, "You gotta spend money to make money." A similar axiom has grown in popularity among facilities professionals: "You gotta spend money to save money." Said another way, "Pay now or pay later." It has been long proven throughout numerous studies and reported in various sources that in addition to some of the non-quantifiable costs mentioned above, unplanned repairs can cost as much as three to four times the cost of effective preventive maintenance. Capital asset management is no different.

As previously articulated about the cost of emergencies, failure to adhere to the established standards of the organization and renew capital assets according to those guidelines, the total cost of ownership of the facilities will increase. Any business case discussion regarding the implementation of an enterprise asset management system must include the juxtaposition of the cost of inaction. By clearly articulating the potential gains of implementing an enterprise asset management system while also comparing and contrasting the cost of inaction, including both the tangible and intangible factors, the officers of the organization will have a more rounded perspective on the potential for the program's success.

Notes to Part I

1 Ibid.
2 Ibid.
3 Rose et al., *Buildings...The Gifts That Keep on Taking*.
4 Christensen, "Recapitalization Management."
5 Rose et al., *Buildings...The Gifts That Keep on Taking*.
6 Ibid.
7 Christensen, "What Is TCO? Why TCO?"
8 Christensen, "Recapitalization Management."
9 Ibid.
10 Ibid.
11 Rose et al., *Buildings...The Gifts That Keep on Taking*.
12 Christensen, Rose, and Ruprecht, "A Common Vocabulary for Asset Investment Strategy."
13 Rose et al., *Buildings...The Gifts That Keep on Taking*.
14 Ibid.
15 Leroy, Medlin, and Glazner, "Vision, People, and Process: An Interview with APPA President Doug Christensen."
16 Ibid.
17 Bennis, *On Becoming a Leader*.
18 Rose et al., *Buildings...The Gifts That Keep on Taking*.
19 Leroy, Medlin, and Glazner, "Vision, People, and Process: An Interview with APPA President Doug Christensen."
20 Rose et al., *Buildings...The Gifts That Keep on Taking*.
21 Ibid.
22 Davenport, "Competing on Analytics."

Part II: Setup

Chapter 4: Organization

"A capital needs program is a critical part of the total maintenance responsibility.
It merges the information from a capital needs study and
integrates within a physical plant operation."
~Douglas K. Christensen[1]

To this point, a lot has been said about the strategic and leadership elements of enterprise asset management. The reason is that any capital needs planning effort must be rooted in a foundation of strategic collaboration with elements of change administration. Without a foundation of a healthy sense of urgency, a strong team, and a shared strategic vision, analysis, assessment, needs projections, or other program outputs run the risk of not being fully understood or appreciated resulting in less than successful administration of the program.

Now that a strategic foundation has been laid, the work of organizing, setting up, and managing the new asset management program can commence. Much of the strategic analysis completed during Part I will prove invaluable during the subsequent parts of this process. It is also important to keep in mind that things change. Maintaining flexibility to adapt to a changing leadership, mission, or expectations will be essential for long-term success.

Ensure Mission Alignment

As was prevalent throughout Part I, the importance of mission alignment cannot be overemphasized. Without aligning the asset management program with the mission, vision, and values of the organization, support will be inconsistent and oftentimes much harder to achieve.

Determining what constitutes "mission alignment" requires much more than a re-reading of the organization's mission statement or strategic plan. While those are important aspects of the exercise, the true character of the organizational strategic mission is multi-faceted and can be spread across several divisions, departments, teams, and committees. Some of the key stakeholders are listed below.

Senior Leadership

Engaging with the senior leadership of the organization is vital to the success of the asset management program. Without aligning the new program with the vision and mission of the senior leaders, the asset management program will, in essence, be a rogue program running parallel to, or even in conflict with, the direction of the organization.

Engineers and Technicians

In many organizations, these "unsung heroes" are vital to any capital planning process. At times, they are overlooked as simply "wrench turners." Yet, these boots-on-the-ground skilled trades men and women know the specific characteristics of the equipment and assets better than any manager, administrator, or consultant. They will know which air handling unit, brand of switchgear, flooring material, or restroom fixtures work best for their facility. While it is true that the laws of thermodynamics are unchanging, the application within the space may be uniquely situated to a particular system, model, or configuration. Only by including those that know the space the best can true mission fit be accomplished.

Budget and Finance
Understanding how the organization's finances work is vital in determining what strategies are best employed in implementing an enterprise asset management process. Some institutions will permit funds to be saved from year to year while other organizations do not. With budget and finance comes procurement. Private organizations tend to have much more flexibility than those in the public sector. Without a firm understanding of funding vehicle options and procurement requirements, capital project plans may be far out of alignment with the policies of the organization. When this happens, asset failures due to under budgeting, lengthy approval processes, and longer than expected lead times can derail the capital strategy resulting in cost overruns, equipment downtime, and customer and organizational impact.

Customers
Engaging customers as stakeholders in the effort can be challenging but is also vital to success. Customer bases can be quite large and engaging all customers is not practical. Instead, engaging a few key customers who have a good breadth of exposure throughout the organization may be a more prudent use of resources than widening the circle and receiving too many opinions.

Customer engagement at this stage requires savvy leadership as it can quickly digress into a recitation of project needs that they "need right now" or "have been waiting for years to get done." What is truly needed at this point is an understanding of how to shape the priorities of the program. The end goal of this interaction should be an understanding of how to prioritize assets and needs as they relate to supporting their efforts to achieve the mission of the organization.

Answer the Five Questions. There is no magic formula for understanding how to best organize and meet the needs of the customer; anyone who says so is selling something. One effective way that has been used to better understand the stakeholders is an exercise known as *The Five Questions. The Five Questions* is an analytical tool developed for continuous improvement that fosters two-way understanding. The five questions are not intended to be rhetorical but actual questions to be answered and intended to help operations consider who they are serving and how best to meet their needs. Additionally, they help to develop a mechanism for garnering feedback needed to redeploy the operation to better meet the needs of the stakeholders.

- **Question 1: Who do we serve and what do they do?**
- **Question 2: What services do they need?**
- **Question 3: How can we know we are doing a great job?**
- **Question 4: What is the best way to provide the services?**
- **Question 5: What is the best way to organize?**

Determine Resource Availability

Similar to the interaction with customers, engaging with the financial stakeholders can quickly digress from the intended purpose into a discussion of what we have in the piggy bank. During an interview in 1999, Doug Christensen affirmed, "The critical lesson we learned from our 1983 study…is that we were focusing on money instead of needs. We were trying to outguess [the] administration on how much money we'd get…**It's better to argue for needs and let administrators determine how to fund them.**"[2]

The program that is being developed is long-range. Financial demands and availability are going to ebb and flow throughout time. What is important to establish in these discussions are the funding vehicles available, not necessarily the available funding of the organization at the present moment. It is essential to know if the organization can hold cash reserves from year to year or if that is not permitted. It is imperative to get a sense of all potential cash resources from which funds can be drawn. It is also important to understand if certain assets have funding limitations based on company policy, trustee control, or legislative appropriations.

The goal of the financial stakeholders, at this point, is to have a baseline understanding of available funding vehicles and determine if holding reserves is an option. If possible, assigning assets to funding responsibilities should also be determined. In a higher education setting, an example may be operating vs. auxiliary funding. However, as some assets may have multiple funding opportunities, that may not be an option. It is important to evaluate all options and have an understanding of what vehicles are possible when decision-making commences.

Establish and Hold to Guiding Principles

As important as strategy, organizational mission, and vision are, any capital planning program needs guiding principles in order to endure. These guiding principles need to be tailored to the individual organization, but they must also be sufficiently flexible in order to adapt to shifting strategic priorities and changes in the overall mission of the organization.

In 1981, the Capital Needs Analysis Center at Brigham Young University articulated and adopted these nine principles to guide their efforts:

1. *Problems are best solved on location right where the problems usually reveal both itself and the solution. Here, problem-solvers have access to the most pertinent information. In order for problems to be solved on location, local problem-solvers must be empowered to act on that information.*
2. *Management skills are most appropriately applied to things. People respond more readily to leadership. Managing a facility is appropriate because a facility is a thing. But if people are between you and the facility, sharpen your leadership skills.*
3. *'I teach them correct principles and they govern themselves.'[3] Leadership inspires doing the right thing. Management focuses on doing the thing right. Leaders teach correct principles and must trust local facility management to responsibly govern themselves in doing the thing right. Bottom-up communication flow.*
4. *Definitive criteria and common standards of judgment evolve through CNA's needs approval process that requires and/or invites multilateral participation and*

perverse perspectives. 'In the mouth of two or three witnesses every word may be established.'[4] 'Where no council is, the people fall; but in the multitude of counselors, there is safety' (The Bible, KJV, Prov. 11:14).

5. *'For all things must be done in order, and by common consent…'[5] In CNA's needs approval process, common consent translates into consensus. Participants in the decision-making process approach differences. Until there is unity, no action is taken.*

6. *Participants in CNA's decision-making process work together in council, and no power or influence can or ought to be maintained by virtue of [rank or position], only by persuasion, by long-suffering, by gentleness and meekness, and by love unfeigned; by kindness and pure knowledge…and without guile.*

7. *It is not wise and is short-sighted to be responsible for assets without understanding the cradle-to-grave impacts on resources. Responsible asset ownership is obligatory. 'For which of you, intending to build a tower, sitteth not down first, and counteth the cost, whether he have sufficient to finish it?'[6]*

8. *Cyclical incidents of capital renewal life-cycle and one-time project needs should be managed in an asset inventory database. This management tool can remember details and prompt timely inspections, track ongoing and changing needs and be a tool to lead and manage the capital needs.*

9. *CNA is built on the concepts of continuous improvement and continuous learning. The ever-improving information and knowledge learned from actual experience must be translated into the database. Refinement of useful life will provide better resource projections and better practices.*

These principles were established in 1981 by the Capital Needs Analysis team at Brigham Young University and remained consistent throughout the years to provide guidance and direction through staffing turnover, leadership changes, and adjustments in strategic priorities. The principles reflected the culture and religious foundation of the university. Establishing similar guiding principles based on the culture and values of the organization can help to ensure the long-term endurance of the capital planning program.

Establish Key Roles

In an effort to effectively administer the program, key positions must be utilized. It is important to share duties and responsibilities. This will engage more people in the process, which will create buy-in and support of the program and decision making. It will also add a breadth of perspective that otherwise would be absent during the process. Lastly, it provides continuity. If a participant or even a leader in the process leaves the organization, the program does not collapse on itself.

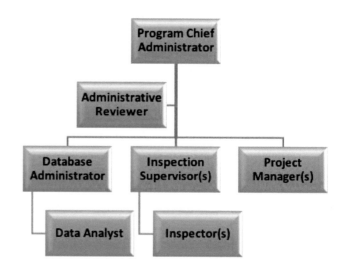

Some possible key positions that should be considered are listed below. These can be full-time individuals, additional roles that current staff take on to support the program, or could employ a different structure entirely. Regardless of the structure and how roles are distributed, it is important that it is articulated and that each individual knows his/her duties and responsibilities in support of the program.

> **Program Chief Administrator** – The program chief administrator is the senior authority over the program. They possess the authority to approve reports and recommendations before they are sent to senior management or administration for review. They assign tasks and make key decisions on areas that may be in dispute. They have complete ownership over the program.

> **Administrative Reviewer** – The administrative reviewer will review assets and systems generally. They will make recommendations based on reasonable expectations and observations. They review recommendations made by inspectors in the context of the master plan and other strategic initiatives. They compile and review reports that are submitted to the program chief administrator.

> **Project Manager** – The project manager is responsible for implementing the project plans from inspection to completion. They review the project proposal from the inspection supervisor and recommend any changes to the program chief administrator. They report to the database administrator and data analyst all required asset data at the completion of the project and confirm the data is accurately reflected in the capital needs reports.

> **Database Administrator** – The database administrator is responsible for maintaining the database and ensuring that all work done maintains the integrity of the data. They also create requested custom reports. They recommend upgrades and database changes based on program administration and needs of the process. The database administrator is not necessarily a facilities professional. While that is helpful, it is more important to have a familiarity with industry concepts and vernacular but also, a deeper understanding of database administration and information systems.

> **Data Analyst** – Working with the database administrator, the data analyst works to add, edit, and update information in the database according to what is reported to them. As with the database administrator, this individual need not be a facilities professional but a familiarity with industry concepts and vernacular is important.

> **Inspection Supervisor** – The inspection supervisor coordinates the work of the annual condition assessment. They assign tasks to the various inspectors that they feel are best qualified to ascertain a proper assessment of a particular asset. They receive the inspection reports and recommendations and review them for accuracy and completeness. They compare them with current activities throughout the operation and make notes of any findings. They work with the inspectors to make recommendations on life-cycle extensions and asset retrofits, repairs, and replacements. They confirm or recommend project priorities in consultation with the inspectors. They develop project recommendations including estimates of soft and hard costs. They prepare reports for the administrative reviewer and the program chief administrator. Inspection supervisors should have an in-depth knowledge of the built environment and ability to discuss key concepts and vernacular without issue.

> **Inspector** – Inspectors are those charged with the physical condition assessment of the asset. They make determinations regarding remaining life and opportunities for retrofit or renewal projects. They make recommendations on replacement units whether that be type-for-type or to alter the duty or intent in any way. They make recommendations on make, model, standard, function, or any other technical aspect of the asset. They confirm if the estimated replacement value is reasonable.

Depending on the size of the organization and the resources available for the program, some organizations will have multiple individuals in each role while others will double-up assigning multiple roles to the same person. It is important to identify within the organization which positions are going to perform the duties irrespective of the individual currently occupying the position. Only by considering the position and not the individual can the structure of the organization be sustainable to continue through multiple generations of staff.

Determine Assessment Level
The last piece that needs to be determined before data gathering work can commence is to determine the assessment level for the program. This assessment level is determined by the amount of resources available to manage the program efficiently. Not every organization has the ability to operate a highly detailed lifetime assessment of all assets.

Various levels of detail and assessment will need to be ascertained for the individual operation. Another strategy is to start with a lesser assessment level, build some data and credibility, and then use that data as support for a recommendation to expand resources and enhance the assessment level and detail. Whatever strategy is determined, it should be sustainable and meet the current availability of resources to be maintainable for years to come.

There are seven basic assessment levels as defined in Table 4.1. Within each of these levels, there are varying levels of detail that can be pursued as needed within the operation. These assessment levels range from no assessment to lifetime assessment.

The most proactive and strategic assessment level is lifetime assessment. However, not all operations have the resources to maintain a fully detailed lifetime assessment model of all assets, systems, and components. Combinations may be required depending on complexity of the systems and resources available. An example of how an operation could utilize multiple assessment levels is as follows:

- **Lifetime Assessment** is used for all major assets such as central plant boilers and chillers, central plant pumps, power substations, and data centers.
- **Life-Cycle Assessment is** used for all minor assets such as building air handling units, rooftop units, pumps, roofing systems, servers, and building-wide or multiple building transformers.
- **Detailed Condition Assessment** is used for all remaining systems and components such as remaining building envelope components, plumbing delivery systems, electrical delivery systems, fiber networks, network switches and routers, restroom fixtures, interior finishes, locks and access controls, and security systems.

Table 4.1

Assessment Level	Definition	Method	Results	Decision Making	Long-Term Plan	Business Fit
No Assessment	No awareness of asset status	None	Emergencies and surprises	Crisis-driven	None	Assets not planned properly
Breakdown Assessment	Wait until asset fails before assessing needs	Communicate failures as they happen	Emergencies and surprises	As needed, at the time	None	Resources not planned properly
Parametric Assessment	Statistical analysis of asset resource needs without inventory details	Detail sample gathering and extrapolating sample results over remaining assets	Global projection of resource needs without specific details	Determines potential investment need	Snapshot of needs based on statistical sampling	Large complex areas that need to know how big the problem is' not fit for managing
General Condition Assessment	A snapshot review of current asset conditions focused on projects needed at the time of assessment.	Visual look at the condition of assets with project scope and cost estimates	A list of projects and priorities that need to be completed	Complete projects identified in the assessment; unplanned failures would be a surprise	Snapshot of needs; typically only projected every 3 to 5 years as needed and as resources become available	Places where a current scope of work, priorities, and cost estimates are needed to improve current assets; little future consideration with assets excluded from assessment
Detailed Condition Assessment	A snapshot review of asset conditions and projections of needs for 3 to 5 years at the time of the assessment	A greater detail review of asset needs, scope, and cost estimates	List of projects and priorities that need to be completed	Complete projects identified in the assessment; unplanned failures would be a surprise	Snapshot of needs; typically only projected every 3 to 5 years as needed and as resources become available	Places where a current scope of work, priorities, and cost estimates are needed to improve current assets; little future consideration with assets excluded from assessment
Life-cycle Assessment	Detailed inventory of assets where life-cycle is tracked and decisions are made on life-cycle	Inventory of all assets, systems, and components; determine remaining life-cycle, set replacement costs, and manage assets according to remaining life-cycle	Annual inspection of all assets, systems, and components where the remaining life-cycle at or below 1 or 2 years remaining determining which need to be refurbished, retrofit, replaced, or are to continue in their current state	Matches high priority assets requiring replacement with limited resource availability weighing the impact of inaction	Inventory allows for long-range projection of asset needs for the life-cycle of all assets managed by the program	Places where projecting the need and level of resources, inspecting current needs, and setting priorities are needed to make good long-term decisions
Lifetime Assessment	Detailed inventory of assets where all costs are tracked and useful life decisions are made	Inventory all assets, systems, and components, set life-cycle and replacement costs, manage remaining life, and track all costs related to the assets	Annual inspection of all assets, systems, and components where the remaining life-cycle is at or below 1 or 2 years determining which assets are to be refurbished, retrofit, replaced, or are to continue in their current state	Matches high priority assets requiring replacement with limited resource availability weighing the impact of inaction while also considering the actual realized cost of maintaining the asset	The inventory and cost tracking allows for projecting the resource and asset needs for the life-cycle of all assets being managed	Places where projecting the needs and level of resources, inspecting current needs, setting high priority needs, and tracking all costs related to assets is needed to make good long-term decisions

Chapter 5: Inventory and Initial Projections

"Defining how far and how much to inventory is a significant part of the study design. Careful consideration as to how much detail to incorporate into the study was of the highest concern."
~Douglas K. Christensen [7]

Now that the organizational framework has been laid, the task of data gathering can commence. Unlike other forms of assessment, it is intended that this physical inventory only be taken once. It will be audited and verified at key strategic points throughout the program; however, the goal is to ensure accuracy of the initial data input. As the old saying goes, "garbage in, garbage out." Inaccurate data can lead to false conclusions and jeopardize the credibility of the program.

Before the physical work of data collection can take place, a few decisions regarding how the data is to be organized need to be made.

Location Hierarchy

To ensure that the data is usable in a total cost of ownership framework, it must be coupled with a location database. Determining how granular of a capital needs program is desired will determine how granular of a location database is needed. For example, if the organization is primarily interested in seeing TCO rollups to the building level, having floor, wing, and room numbers subdivided out may be unnecessary work. However, the organization may have facilities spread across several different geographies and understanding the various TCOs of each building, campus, or geographical reference would be key in decision making. An example of a global location hierarchy is illustrated in Figure 5.1[8]. Here is another area where alignment of the strategic mission is key. Understanding how the organization reviews and interprets data will help to determine the level of granularity that will be the most valuable.

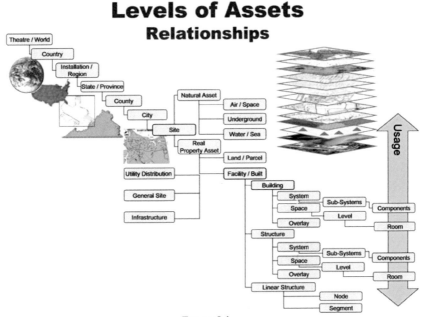

Figure 5.1
Global Location Hierarchy

Managed Asset Selection

Just as it was important to select the assessment level during the organization phase, it is now time to select the assets to be managed as part of the program. This list can start small to only include those critical assets and systems requiring the most attention and then expand as more resources are made available to support the program. When describing the establishment of the BYU CNA Center in his 1986 Rex Dillow Award winning article, "Integrating Capital Studies within Physical Plant Organizations," Doug Christensen described the importance of selecting the right level of assets:

> *Defining how far and how much to inventory is a significant part of the study design. Careful consideration as to how much detail to incorporate into the study was of the highest concern. We struggled and settled on a level that would give enough information to manage replacements.*[9]

There are two key elements to be taken into consideration when evaluating how detailed of an inventory to pursue. The first is how to roll up the geographic data. What is the finest level of data and how will it roll up? Will it start at the room level and then roll to the building, campus, region, then global organization or some other way?

As an example, when BYU established their location hierarchy, they inventoried the rooms but then summarized the room data by room type (i.e., classroom, office, corridor, mechanical, etc.), followed by floor and building. Doug Christensen further explained in his article, "An example: we would not replace carpet in one office but would consider all of the offices on a single floor within a building. When all of the offices on that floor needed carpet replacements, we would replace *all* of the carpet."[10]

The second element to consider when evaluating the level of detail is with regard to the utility systems. When completing the initial inventory, many of the assets in a particular system will have similar, if not the same, installation dates as well as life-cycles. For example, in HVAC, the chiller, boiler, air handling unit, chilled and heating water supply lines, ductwork, and controls may all have been installed on the same date; however, many of these systems would have different life-cycles.

As another example of how this was set up by the BYU CNA Center, assets with similar life-cycles would be grouped into a system while the major assets with differing life-cycles would be separated out. The chillers and air handling units would be assigned their specific life-cycle, while the supply lines, duct work, and electrical delivery would be grouped into an asset system and renewed accordingly.

This method of summarizing assets into systems and geographic areas helps to avoid unnecessary details as well as confusion when evaluating assets for retrofit, renewal, or replacement. Specific strategies should be taken into consideration in the context of the mission of the organization and the specific needs of the assets.

Classification

While gathering data, it is important to know how to classify and name the data that is being collected. Some organizations, if they are state or federally funded, are required to use a particular classification system such as OmniClass, Uniformat II, ASTM FACTS, or another industry established classification hierarchy. If that is required, it is recommended to utilize those classification methods while conducting the inventory.

If the required format does not meet the needs of the organization and a different or home-grown method is preferred, a cross-reference database should be developed in order to provide clarity when reporting back to the governing body. With many databases, a user-defined field can be utilized to accommodate the dual-classification system.

If no specific classification is required, it is best to evaluate several options as well as in-house developed methods to determine which will work best and provide the most intuitive classification groupings. Whatever classification system is used, it is important to be consistent and accurate to ensure accurate reporting and analysis.

Asset Nomenclature

To identify the individual assets, each one must have a unique identifier. Hundreds or even thousands of records will be created during the inventory process; and it is important to be able to identify the asset, as clearly as possible, by the name that it is given. A popular format that is used throughout the industry is:

Building – Classification – Serial

As an example, the asset name of an air handling unit in the Administration Building might look something like this:

AB – AHU – 01

AB – Administration Building
AHU – Air Handling Unit
01 – Serial Number 01

There are any number of possibilities when it comes to naming assets. It may be valuable to incorporate a campus or other geographic reference as well for organizations that are spread across multiple areas. As with classification, there are many ways to make this happen. The key is to be accurate and consistent.

Asset Prioritization

In a world with limited resources, all things must be prioritized. Capital assets are no different. There are assets that would close buildings in the event of a single failure and others where building occupants wouldn't even notice. Establishing a common, objective means of prioritizing assets will prove valuable when replacement planning comes up. Having an asset prioritization strategy developed and approved will also help to avoid less important assets to be promoted in the priority because of political influence.

There are multiple ways to develop a prioritization strategy. It is important to develop what works best for the organization. The most important key to consider is how the priorities support the overall mission. If they support the goals and objectives of the physical facilities operation but do not consider the overall mission, the priorities will not be supported when difficult decisions need to be made regarding allocation of resources. An effective prioritization strategy will do both.

Prioritization strategies can either be complex taking a multitude of weighted factors into consideration or they can be much a simpler matrix similar to the one below.

Critical	Area served by the asset is closed at first failure. Potential safety risk upon failure. Considerable financial impact. No redundancy.
High	Some redundancy. Short-term stop-gap measures are available but not for extended periods of time.
Moderate	Redundancy exists and failures could be absorbed for one, maybe two fiscal cycles.
Low	Redundancy exists or is not needed. Minor or no discomfort if the asset fails.

Whatever prioritization method is used, it is vital that it is agreed upon during the setup phase of establishing the new program. If priorities are not discussed until the first reports, decision makers will be swayed by the juxtaposition of only the assets listed for replacement rather than the comprehensive context of the strategic objectives of the asset management program.

Database Selection

Before embarking on collecting data, it is important to identify where all the records will be stored. The database is a key part of this process. Most organizations select the application and then adapt their business practices to the software. That method is the direct opposite of what is recommended.

Before a database can be selected, some introspection must be conducted. As referenced in Part I, an understanding of the results the organization desires and the key processes that are undertaken must be understood. Only when those things are known can database selection begin. Other questions, such as classification, nomenclature, granularity, location, and summarization must be asked when determining if a database is the right fit. Granted, there will be some shifting of minor processes in order to accommodate database tasks. However, the primary objectives and goals of the organization must be supported in full by the database; otherwise, it will not be an effective tool in meeting the needs of the capital planning process.

There are many databases throughout the industry that can meet the desired objectives of the capital planning process. Some questions to consider are:

- ✓ Does it have all the data points that are needed to make wise decisions?
- ✓ Does it have the ability to utilize the chosen classification method?
- ✓ Does it have the ability to integrate the selected nomenclature system?
- ✓ Does it have an integrated work order module, or will it communicate to the work order system currently in place?

- ✓ Does it have attached documents such as construction drawings, specifications, and inspection reports?
- ✓ Does it have the ability to summarize asset histories?
- ✓ Does it have the ability to summarize assets by classification and locations by type?
- ✓ Is customization of the database possible?
- ✓ Are there fees for customization of the database?
- ✓ Is the data exportable to an MS Excel, MS Access, or other desired format?
- ✓ Can it produce custom reports based on the organization's unique needs?
- ✓ Is it affordable?
- ✓ Is the price competitive with companies that offer similar solutions?
- ✓ Is the end-user interface intuitive, or does it require considerable training?
- ✓ Is the data stored on-site or in "the cloud"?
- ✓ What updates are required and how frequently?
- ✓ How are updates administered?

Inventory Collection

Now that the foundation of what to name the assets, how to classify the assets, how to prioritize the assets, and where to store the data has been established, the task of the physical collection of data can proceed. The nuts and bolts of how best to complete this is different for every operation. Collection can be completed building by building or system by system. The how-to matters little except that the process should be efficient, effective, and consistent. If the database selected is mobile-ready, gathering the data can be streamlined and entered right into the system. If not, surveyors must be thorough and write clearly; otherwise, there could be an increase of rework and data entry errors resulting in inaccurate information.

One best practice to consider is to have the shop responsible for the assets collect the data and conduct an initial condition assessment while they survey. This will require the data gathering to be more organized, and training will need to be conducted. But having electricians inspect panels, plumbers inspect pumps, and carpenters inspect roofs has the potential to provide a much more thorough and accurate assessment than an administrator who does not work with those systems day in and day out.

Trust needs to be extended to allow competent, skilled individuals to make these assessments. If they are truly not situated to make these assessments because of skillset or competency, alternative means can be explored. However, if that is the case, the technicians should still continue to participate in the survey so they can have the opportunity to get exposure to the program as well as provide input where possible. This effort to include the shops, along with providing professional development training to get employees in position to make these assessments, will yield dividends and lower the cost of program administration.

Critical data points that should be gathered for this initial inventory are as follows:

- ✓ Asset Identifier
- ✓ Description
- ✓ Classification Identifier

- ✓ System
- ✓ Location
- ✓ Installation Date
- ✓ Life-cycle
- ✓ Remaining Life
- ✓ Size or Quantity of Asset
- ✓ Unit of Measure
- ✓ Priority
- ✓ Current Replacement Cost per Unit
- ✓ Current Total Replacement Value

Some "nice to have" data points that should also be gathered if possible are as follows:
- ✓ Manufacturer
- ✓ Model Number
- ✓ Serial Number
- ✓ Initial Planning and Design Costs
- ✓ Initial Installation Cost
- ✓ Projected Disposal Cost
- ✓ Repair Histories
- ✓ Energy Consumption Histories
- ✓ Estimated Remaining Useful Life (*if different from life-cycle*)
- ✓ Estimated Remaining Investment Life (*if different from life-cycle*)

Initial Projections

Now that the data has been gathered and compiled, the next step of the process is to calculate the initial projections and identify the estimated annual funding needs for the new capital needs analysis program. The capital needs projection (see Figure 5.2) is a bar chart of the aggregate current replacement values of all the assets that are forecast for replacement in the indicated year.

One key to effectiveness with this projection is the length of the forecast. Condition assessments would typically only look forward five or ten years. This limited perspective creates challenges when forecasting funding needs. It is recommended that a projection timeline of 30 or 40 years be considered to capture life-cycles that are longer and may be outside the projection timeline.

As an example, if a chiller has a 30-year life-cycle and it is currently five years into its life, a 10- or 20-year projection would not capture that asset within the timeframe. In the five-year condition assessment way of thinking, that was fine. Capital plans and funding analyses were not submitted for more than 20 years in the future, if that long. By projecting out 40 years, that chiller would then be included in the analytics and bigger picture assessment. In a more strategic life-cycle capital needs analysis, the longer timeline becomes a more significant factor. The financial impact of the projecting timeline will be addressed in more detail in the next section.

It is important to remember that, at this point, this is only a preliminary projection. This is only the data that has been gathered with little or no assessment. It is hopeful that some assessment was gathered while conducting the initial survey of the assets. However, as will be discussed in Chapter 7, a more detailed assessment of the condition of the assets and evaluation of remaining life will be conducted during the "Zero Tour."

Projected Annual Funding

The point at which the projection timeframe becomes important is in the estimated annual funding of the program. Figure 5.2 shows a trend graph from the BYU CNA Center. This chart shows, to the left, the actual needs juxtaposed with the appropriations and, to the right, the 40-year projected replacement needs of the four campuses included in the program. Where the timeline becomes important, and why this method of capital planning can be more strategic than the old five-year condition assessment model, is found in the yellow line.

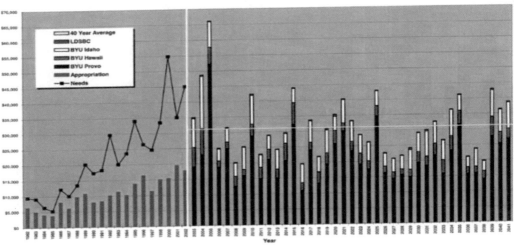

Figure 5.2
Projected Annual Funding

The yellow line shown in Figure 5.2 is an estimated average of the funding needs over the next 40 years. As shown in the chart, the aggregate current replacement values vary from year to year. They really can't even be defined as cyclical. There are peaks as high as $65 million and valleys as low as $20 million. Submitting capital funding requests that swing $45 million from year to year can be quite challenging, to say the least.

Rather than submitting funding requests with such a wide-sweeping range, funding all capital needs replacements with one annual funding limit is more palatable and strategic. In Figure 5.2, the yellow line indicating BYU's funding limit is approximately $31 million. This $31 million is, quite simply, the 40-year average of annual needs. The concept is simple. Each year, this $31 million is funded into the CNA account. What is approved as a CNA project is funded from this account. Funds that are not used are held in arrears for when they are needed.

In its infancy, unless the facilities included are less than 10 years old, the capital needs program will likely require more than the estimated annual funding limit in order to meet the projected replacement needs. At that point, two strategic questions should be asked.

1. Can we afford a cash infusion into the program to help "catch up" on our deferred capital renewal? If so, how much will we require to meet the needs of the critical assets?
2. What assets are not critical and can be deferred to later years when the aggregate funding need is lower than our estimated funding limit?

A strategy consisting of a balance of those two questions will provide the ability to "catch up" and bring the program back into sync with the average funding need. For the first five or ten years, these two questions may need to be asked again if the projected need exceeds the available funding.

Chapter 6: Program Quality Assurance

*"Facilities Management is People Management
and we bring the buildings along for laughs."*
~Douglas K. Christensen

As has been often stated, "garbage in, garbage out." Data and analytics are only as good as what goes into the system. During the inventory phase, great care was taken to ensure that the data was as accurate as possible. As the efforts of program administration commence and more hands get involved in the work, it is important to maintain the integrity of the data.

While the "Internet of Things" has come a long way, there is still a human element that must be considered whenever initiatives like this are pursued. People, regardless of how dedicated and well-meaning, can provide inaccurate data leading to erroneous decisions if not properly trained.

In order to provide training, the information to be taught must first be determined. Just as they are developed for the built environment, standards of database administration need to be established to ensure quality execution of the program. Once standards and expectations are established, a training program can be developed and administered. Lastly, as part of program administration, it is vital to implement checkpoints to verify that training is effective, standards and expectations are being met, and the data is able to be used to reach accurate conclusions. The intersection of these three element—standards, training, and verification—constitutes effective quality assurance (see Figure 6.1).

Figure 6.1
Effective Quality Assurance

Standards

Much of what is to be established as standards has already been addressed earlier in the text. Every operation is different along with the standards and definitions. Some typical items to define in standardization are:

- Process flowcharts
- Database management and utilization
- Database reports
- Assessment levels
- Key data points for inventory
- Standard current replacement values by asset classification
- Standard life-cycles by asset classification
- Asset classification format
- Asset identification nomenclature
- Data collection process
- Asset inspection process and documentation
- Annual condition assessment process
- Decision making process
- Funding request process

All these factors work toward establishing a standard of data management that must be documented and used in training all staff in administration of the program. Not all of them will be known at the beginning of the journey. The standards manual is intended to be a living document that is updated regularly; at minimum, during the annual review process.

Throughout the process of setup and implementation, many of these items are considered and discussed. It is essential to document the standards that are decided upon and incorporate them into a standards manual for future reference. Not every operation will have dedicated capital asset managers that will work with the data and database every day. Many will be reliant on a manager or director taking on enterprise asset management as part of their other duties. In those cases, interaction with the data and database will likely be more infrequent.

Not having a clearly articulated standard with definitions will create inconsistencies in the methodology and skew data. Only by documenting processes and lessons learned can the operation become a true learning organization and improve from year to year.

Training Development and Administration
More than once, a new program has been successfully rolled out and implemented only to have it collapse from a single point of failure. Using the defined standards, training programs will then need to be developed and implemented to ensure the new program will prove resilient for generations of staff that will participate.

Chapter 10 will review the periodic tasks that are required to maintain the program throughout the year. An effective training program will take into account each of those tasks, the standards that each task is expected to maintain, and the individuals responsible for them. Arguably the most important element of the asset management program is to ensure that training is conducted. Without effective training, the data integrity is called into question and inconsistencies arise in the process and outcomes.

Quality Assurance Verification
Even with established standards and effectively administered training, the human element is always a factor that must be considered. As stated previously, regardless of how careful, dedicated, or detail-oriented a person is, mistakes can still happen. Therefore, it is essential that quality assurance safeguards are implemented so that these errors are caught and corrected.

Standard Operating Procedures Handbook. The standard operating procedures handbook (SOP) is the informational clearinghouse for all standards and data elements throughout the program. It is essential that it is maintained and referenced regularly. It includes all foundational analyses and decisions discussed in Part I. It will include all setup elements in Part II. It will also include all the procedural elements and forms used to administer the program as detailed in Part III.

Audit. The details of the database audit will be addressed in Chapter 10. This is a mechanism that will audit 30% of the database annually for accuracy. If the data conducted in that audit is less than 90% accurate, all assets within that classification are audited and corrected as needed.

Reference Sheets. Regardless of how effectively the training is administered, memories fade and it is good to have a reference sheet to remind the individual of the proper procedures. These need not be confined to only critical tasks but should be considered for all elements within the database.

Dual Verification. For critical points of data, namely asset ID, classification, life-cycle, installation date, size, and current replacement value, database updates should require a secondary verification to approve the update. Depending on the database, this function may need to take place outside of the software, but integration into the programming is best, if possible. Regardless, ensuring that a life-cycle or replacement value isn't inadvertently changed is of paramount importance, as the critical points can have a considerable impact on future program administration.

By working to ensure that program quality assurance is maintained, outcomes and longevity of the program will be supported by the users and benefactors. Ensuring that effective but maintainable standards are successfully incorporated into training procedures and then verified periodically by routine checks and balances, the asset management program will be able to maintain the credibility to endure even the closest scrutiny.

Notes to Part II

[1] Christensen, "Capital Needs Analysis Principles."
[2] Rose, *Charting a New Course for Campus Renewal*.
[3] Taylor, "The Organization of the Church."
[4] *The Doctrine and Covenants*.
[5] Ibid.
[6] "Luke 14:28."
[7] Christensen, "Integrating Capital Studies within Physical Plant Operations."
[8] Source: Dana K. Smith, FAIA, DKS Information Consulting, LLC: Used with Permission
[9] Christensen, "Recapitalization Management."
[10] Christensen, "Standing on Shoulders."

Part III: Administration

Chapter 7: Zero Tour Condition Assessment

*"We have learned that, as management and inspectors work together,
a standard for replacements can be agreed upon."*
~Douglas K. Christensen[1]

Up to this point, a lot of data has been gathered and some surface-level assessments have been made. The assets now reside as records in the database ready for the analytics that lead to wise decision making.

This analytical process is started by conducting a "Zero Tour." This tour is a detailed condition assessment of all assets with remaining life that will be at *zero* in the evaluation period. For most, capital needs assessments are conducted during the year prior to when the funding would be allocated. Therefore, the Zero Tour would include all assets with current remaining life of one year or less. If the request cycle is longer, the Zero Tour would simply expand the criteria for the assets to include more years of remaining life.

As mentioned in Chapter 6 on quality assurance, processes and procedures unique to the organization should be documented and training conducted regularly. That being said, there are some key best practices that should be followed, while the individual process may vary from operation to operation.

Pre-Inspection Administrative Review

Prior to the Zero Tour, it is important to conduct an administrative review. This process is detailed in Chapter 9. If this is the first Zero Tour of the new program, an abbreviated administrative review should complete the following activities:

1. Auditing 30% of the assets in each classification. If any of the classification audits yield an accuracy rate of less than 90%, the entire classification should be audited and evaluated for accuracy.
2. Conducting a review of all assets with remaining life of less than five years for reasonableness and life-cycles adjusted where appropriate. This review is not for decision making or assessment. It is merely to determine if the remaining life is reasonable based on the information at hand.

Inspection Preparations

Once the administrative review has been completed, the database administrator will provide the records of all assets with remaining life of one year or less. They should also, where available, provide all records of repair, preventive maintenance, energy consumption, upgrades, retrofits, and other work done on the asset. How these records are provided will vary from operation to operation. Some may prefer written forms. Others may have the ability to conduct inspection and view information using mobile devices. Regardless of what method works best, what is to be provided and how should be documented.

The Zero Tour asset records will be provided to the inspection supervisor who will then review each of the assets for accuracy. They will also organize the inspections so the inspectors most qualified to make sound judgments are assigned those respective assets. This organizational grouping may be by building, by trade, by both, or some other criteria unique to the shop. Whatever the organizational method, it is imperative that the inspector has the technical expertise, decision-making skills, and asset history required to thoroughly evaluate the asset.

Once organized, the inspection supervisor will dispatch the assessments to the inspectors. It is also recommended that s/he provide any technical documents that may help, such as drawings, schematics, specifications, and original equipment manufacturer (OEM) manuals. The inspection supervisor and inspector should also discuss means and methods of how the assessment will be conducted. Will destructive testing be completed, or will it only be non-destructive? Will specialists be retained to conduct portions of the assessment? What resources are available to measure, such as thermal imaging, vibration analysis, ultrasonic testing, etc.? Having a clear understanding of what is expected before the inspections begin will help to avoid re-inspection due to insufficient data.

Inspection

It is important to note, as it has been throughout this text, that the individuals to complete the physical inspection portion of the condition assessment should be those who have the most intimate knowledge of the asset and are charged with maintaining and operating the asset. Having an administrator inspect dynamic equipment, as an example, would not be as effective because the engineering team that works with the equipment every day will have far better history, context, and perspective of what the true condition and projected remaining life of the equipment is than an administrator, regardless of background.

It can be difficult for some administrators to place their trust of such important inspections with those on the front lines. In order to have an effective condition assessment with the most accurate results, that mindset must be set aside and trust must be developed. Likewise, the inspectors must be cognizant of their own limitations and be willing to admit when something is beyond their skillset. In his 1986 article titled "Integrating Capital Studies Within Physical Plant Operations," Doug Christensen said,

> *Employees from the maintenance shops are the inspectors and provide management with information based from a maintenance point of view. . . . The great advantage to shops doing the inspections is the tying together of all maintenance information. We have learned that, as management and inspectors work together, a standard for replacements can be agreed upon.*[2]

By maintaining an open dialog of candid, respectful communication, administrators, supervisors, and technicians can come together and achieve the desired results with much more accurate outcomes.

Once the inspectors have been charged with their inspections and assigned the assets they are to inspect, they shall proceed to conduct the condition assessment of those assets. Before starting the physical inspection of the assets, the inspectors should also take time to review each of the assets in their charge for accuracy. They may have first-hand knowledge that an asset was replaced recently, failed recently, is scheduled for replacement, is part of a renovation plan, or other factors that may negate the need to conduct an inspection. That information should be noted and reported to the inspection supervisor as part of the inspection process.

After the review of the assets is completed, the physical condition assessment can commence. Several factors should be evaluated while conducting the inspection. Some examples are listed in Table 7.1. Detailed inspection checklists should be developed based on the specific needs of the organization.

Table 7.1

General Items...	Architectural Elements...	Dynamic Equipment...
✓ Safety Concerns ✓ Functionality ✓ Performing as Designed ✓ Meeting the Intended Use ✓ Meeting the Current Needs ✓ Visual Inspection of General Condition ✓ Remaining Warranty	✓ Stains or Wear Patterns ✓ Separated Seams or Rippling ✓ Missing Grout ✓ Outdated Aesthetically ✓ Tiles Broken or Missing ✓ Missing or Cracked Veneer ✓ Standing Water on Roofs ✓ Drains in Good Repair ✓ Unwanted Vegetation ✓ Functioning Windows ✓ Thermal Intrusion ✓ Moisture Intrusion	✓ General Function ✓ Vibration Analysis ✓ Thermal Imaging ✓ Energy Consumption ✓ Piping and Valves ✓ Safety Devices ✓ Cabling and Insulation ✓ Failed Components ✓ Availability of Replacement Parts ✓ Refrigerant Type

Consultants
It may be required to hire consultants to conduct a portion of the assessment. It is important to note that the consultants are approaching the situation with little to no context of the history, intended use, or idiosyncrasies of the equipment. It is vitally important that the inspector charged with that particular asset, and all other technicians that are familiar with the asset, be engaged in supporting the consultant. With background information, the consultant can provide a more thorough assessment of the condition of the asset.

Inspector's Report
Once the assessment of an asset is completed, the inspectors shall compile all their findings, including measurements, history, and future plans into one report. It is typically most effective to provide a common format to report the information. Thus, if there are multiple inspectors, they all provide the desired information in the format that is clear and understood by the inspection supervisors.

Inspection Supervisor's Review
Following the completion of the inspector's assessment, the inspector and inspection supervisor discuss the findings. They review the data and compile the information in preparation for the decision-making process. They complete another review of any master plans, strategic plans, or construction plans in development to confirm if there are any assets that are part of their report that are being programmed for replacement or upgrade. Once the inspector and inspection supervisor have a comfort level with the information pertaining to the assets, they can begin the decision-making process.

Chapter 8: Zero Tour Condition Assessment Evaluation

"The [Data Maturity Model] is a model of how organizations need to gather data and share the results, but in the information age, it is critical that we turn information into what it is telling us."
~Douglas K. Christensen [3]

Within the Data Maturity Model, data is the foundation of good decision making but that data must be compiled in such a way that the information can be used to make knowledgeable decisions leading to understanding and wisdom.[4]

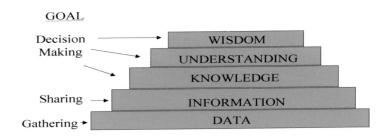

Figure 8.1
Data Maturity Model

To further illustrate this evolution and what the end goal should be, the Data Refinement Model (Figure 8.2) offers some assistance. It effectively explains the differences within the different levels of the model.[5] Now that the Zero Tour data has been organized into usable information, it is ready to be validated. Throughout the decision-making process it is important to keep an eye on what is needed to advance understanding by applying knowledge and experience. The next step is to move on to wisdom by making good judgments based on reliable, meaningful, and useful information.

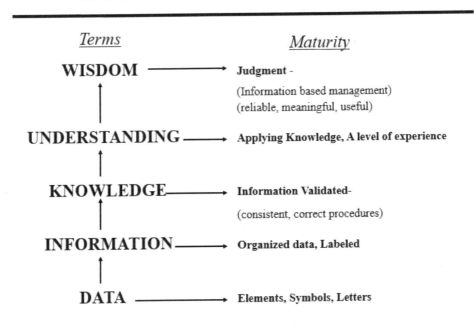

Figure 8.2
Data Refinement Model

Asset Recommendations

Following the inspection, the inspector and inspection supervisor work together to compile their recommended actions for each asset. Their recommendations will fall into one of seven categories:

Extend. For assets that are functioning well and for which preventive maintenance will continue to be effective, the decision may be to *extend* the life-cycle. It will be the determination of the inspector with the support of the inspection supervisor to determine the number of years the asset's life-cycle will be extended.

Whatever the extension is, those additional years should be noted and used to adjust the standard life-cycle of this asset in this duty. As an example, if a standard life-cycle of a fan-coil unit in an office is typically 15 years but this particular asset has received two years of life-cycle extensions, when the asset is finally replaced, the new original life-cycle of the asset in this location should be 17. Inversely, if the standard life-cycle was 15 and it failed two years prematurely, the replacement asset should have an original life-cycle of 13 years.

Many factors impact the actual realized life-cycle of an asset: frequency of preventive maintenance, quality of repairs, quality of the original manufacturing, and environment. Adjusting the life-cycles in this manner will help to capture the unique environmental impact on the life-cycle of each asset.

Repair. Some assets, when inspected, will reveal that minor repairs may need to be made, but otherwise, the asset remains functional. Any work noted that extends the life of the asset less than five years should be categorized as a repair. These actions typically do little to extend the life of the asset but rather keep it in its current functional state and on track with its original life-cycle. That being said, if the asset is at 0 years remaining life and it only needs some minor repairs, it is safe to assume that the repairs will be accompanied by a life-cycle extension of some sort. The inspector should report back the precise repairs that need to be made and the estimated life-cycle extension to accompany the repairs. This work could commence immediately as this would logically be funded out of the operating budget.

Renew. There will be assets that are not yet ready for replacement but are also in need of more work than a simple repair. Provided the asset is still generally maintaining its intended use and is not more costly to own than to replace, a more extensive renewal effort may be in order. Asset renewal would consist of more comprehensive and invasive work to return the asset closer to a more functional state. As a general rule, asset renewals should only be explored if the accompanying life-cycle gain is five years or greater. If a minimum of five years cannot be obtained, serious evaluation should be considered as to whether a replacement strategy is more fitting.

Retrofit. Some assets may no longer meet the intended use of the design and require work to bring it in line with its mission-driven purpose. This work is referred to as a retrofit. An example of this would be an air handling unit designed to handle the heating and cooling load of a standard classroom but that classroom has now been converted to a computer lab. The cooling capacity may be insufficient to handle the heat gain of the students as well as the computers. Rather than replace the unit, this may be resolved with a retrofit of the AHU.

As with asset renewal, a minimum threshold of five years of gained life should be a standard that is held to. With anything less than five years, an evaluation of the cost versus benefit should be considered.

Replace – End of Investment Life. A key point in the deliberation to replace any asset is value. Managers must ask themselves, "Am I spending more to maintain this asset than it is worth?" Many factors go into this decision. Some are listed below, but understand that every organization is different and there may be other valuable costs not listed.

- Cost of preventive maintenance activities
- Cost of repairs
- Frequency of repairs
- Cost of downtime during repairs
- Opportunity cost of energy use juxtaposed with a new unit to do the same duty

In addition to the hard costs are the intangible costs, which are difficult to quantify. These may be things like institutional reputation, customer satisfaction, quality of instruction in the classrooms, productivity of the staff, and other similar impacts that may influence a decision. For this point, however, only tangible costs will be considered.

In these cases, where the asset is functioning well and meeting the design intent but is costing more to keep than to replace, the asset has reached the end of its investment life-cycle. When determining if an asset has reached the end of investment life, there is a simple rule of thumb that can be followed. Keep in mind, the bottom-line question is if the asset costs more to maintain than it is worth. If it costs more to operate than the estimated replacement value, it may be worth replacing. This scenario is rare and typically only arises with dynamic equipment. A simple rule of thumb to determine if the asset may be costing you more to keep than replace is below.

$$(CRV/Life\text{-}cycle) < (Monthly\ Operating\ Costs)$$

Example: Assuming an asset's current replacement value is $10,000 and has a 10-year life-cycle, the annual replacement cost for the asset is $1,000. If the maintenance and operation costs average more than $1,000 per month, the asset is not worth keeping.[6]

Other opportunities to replace an asset that has reached the end of investment life are when doing so can create a considerable return on that investment. This is typically considered for high energy consuming equipment and the project is packaged more as an energy conservation measure (ECM) rather than a capital needs replacement. Regardless of the package, the outcome of the investment strategy is the same: replacement of capital assets.

For projects that potentially could pay for themselves or provide a return on investment, other financial metrics should be incorporated into the evaluation process to ensure the project is going to yield the desired benefit. Two of the more common metrics are listed below:

Simple Payback

Simple payback is one of the more common metrics used to calculate the benefit of an investment strategy. Very simply, it is the number of years it will take for the yield to break even with the investment. As an example, consider the following assumptions about a 100-horsepower pump replacement:

100 Horsepower Pump

Asset Current Replacement Value	$10,000
Asset Life-Cycle	20 Years
Asset Current Age	16 Years
Remaining Life	4 Years
Estimated Annual Maintenance Savings	$780
Estimated Annual Energy Savings	$2,890

Using simple payback, the payback on this project is 2.72 years. Because the payback period is less than the remaining life, it may be worth considering as an investment replacement.

$$\$10,000 \text{ Project Cost} / \$3,670 \text{ Savings per Year} = 2.72 \text{ Years}$$

This is an effective metric in any facility professional's toolbox. While simple to understand and easy to calculate, it does have limitations. Most notably, it does not consider the time value of money or the opportunity cost of pursuing other investment strategies. To capture those factors, a discounted payback should be considered.

Discounted *Payback*

A discounted payback is very similar to a simple payback but, as stated, it takes the time value of money, as well as the opportunity cost of other investment strategies, into consideration. This metric is not typically used in the public sector or not-for-profit organizations as the cost of capital and competing investment strategies are less common.

While similar in nature, calculating a discounted payback is more complex than a simple payback. The first step in this effort is to determine the discount rate. Many organizations use the weighted average cost of capital as their discount rate. Some simply use the current rate of return on the stock market as their opportunity cost. Organizations in education and nonprofit sectors may use the rate of return in the endowment fund as the discount rate. It is important to determine how the organization calculates this percentage. The finance office or chief financial officer may be the best resource in determining this figure.

The next step is to determine the project's cash flows. Using the project assumptions for the simple payback, the cost of capital is now also added:

100 Horsepower Pump

Asset Current Replacement Value	$10,000
Asset Life-cycle	20 Years
Asset Current Age	17 Years
Remaining Life	3 Years
Estimated Annual Maintenance Savings	$780
Estimated Annual Energy Savings	$2,890
Cost of Capital	7.5%

First, the investment time must be broken down into time periods, in this case years. The estimated remaining life is three years, and that will be set as the project target timeframe to determine if early replacement from an investment perspective is financially viable. In addition to the outflows and savings, the discounted cash flows must be calculated. That is calculated as follows:

$$\text{Discounted Cash Flow} = \text{Cash Flow} / (1 + \text{Cost of Capital})^{\text{Year}}$$

Year	Cash Flow	Formula	Discounted Cash Flow	Cumulative Total
Year 0	(10,000)	$-10,000/(1+.075)^0$	(10,000)	(10,000)
Year 1	3,670	$3,670/(1+.075)^1$	3,498	(6,502)
Year 2	3,670	$3,670/(1+.075)^2$	3,254	(3,249)
Year 3	3,670	$3,670/(1+.075)^3$	3,027	(222)
Year 4	3,670	$3,670/(1+.075)^4$	2,815	2,593

In the example with the simple payback, this asset replacement payback period was 2.72 years and considered a viable option for replacement as an investment strategy. When the cost of capital and time value of money is taken into consideration, the payback would not be realized until into the fourth year of the investment, one year after replacing the asset at the end of its life. When considering the discounted payback period, this project would not be considered a viable option as an investment strategy.

These two examples reflect the importance of understanding how the organization views money. If the finance office considers a portfolio of investment strategies and weighs the cost of capital in those decision-making efforts, discounted payback should be used. If not, a simple payback model may be sufficient.

Other means of calculating the value of a project include internal rate of return (IRR), return on investment (ROI), and net present value (NPV). Each method has its pros and cons. It is important that whatever method is used to determine if an asset is a candidate for replacement due to end of investment life, the same method is used for all assets so as to ensure a common assessment of the decision-making criteria.

Replace – End of Useful Life. As organizational missions shift to meet the changing demands of their customers, so facilities evolve as well. In doing so, assets working to meet the mission need to also adapt to these changing conditions. Over the course of the life of an asset, the designed intent of the asset may have changed. There are sometimes occasions when retrofitting an asset can preserve remaining life and keep the asset in place for several more years. However, sometimes retrofits are not an option.

When an asset is no longer serving the mission of the organization, regardless of whether the asset is functioning as designed, it is considered at the end of its useful life.[7] A more direct question might be, "Is the asset doing what we need it to do?" If the answer is "No," the end of useful life may be at or near its end. A common example of assets being replaced at the end of their useful life is computers. Rarely are computers used until the components fail and the system stops working. More often, the computer is replaced because of obsolescence and the fact that technology has evolved to a point where the computer is no longer useful.

There is no magic formula for this, just common sense. In evaluating the asset and discussing the needs with the customers, if it is determined it is not effectively serving the organization, it is best replaced with an asset that will meet the needs of the organization.

Replace – End of Life-cycle. When the asset starts to enter a period where the risk of permanent failure is imminent, the asset is at the end of its life-cycle. This happens when the asset is worn out and comprehensive repairs or retrofits would be required to restore it to its intended functional use.[8] It is at this point where, if the decision is made against replacement, the asset transitions to a deferred capital renewal backlog. Assets at the end of their life must be prioritized for available funding resources based on impact on the institution in the event the asset fails. Those having a greater impact (i.e., health and safety, class cancelations, closed campus, etc.) should be given the highest priority and funding consideration.

This is the phase of asset replacement that is most desirable to avoid. When assets reach this phase, the risk of failure increases and emergency repairs are more expensive than planned repairs. In addition, the cost of downtime, impact of facility operations, and institutional reputation are all factors that come into play at this stage of the life-cycle decision. While there are scenarios where this type of asset investment management is warranted, these decisions should be made strategically in concert with the asset comprehensive plan to avoid potential emergency situations.

Asset Decision Recommendations
Once the inspector and inspection supervisor have agreed on recommendations for each of the assets on their Zero Tour, they compile that information into a report for the administrative reviewer and program chief administrator to review. Ideally, the data that was used to come to those decisions would be contained within the database and the data analyst and database administrator can assist with compiling it and generating the standard reports that are used in the organization.

Following a review of the recommendations by the inspector and inspection supervisor, the program chief administrator will hold an assessment review council with the administrative reviewers, inspection supervisors, inspectors and other key stakeholders that may be able to provide valuable information. This meeting has several objectives.

First is to review all the information submitted and ensure that the principles used in conducting the condition assessment were consistent and in line with the standards and training established in the operation.

Second, it is to evaluate the assigned priorities of the assets and confirm that no changes have been made that would amend the priority levels. For example, if, while conducting the initial inventory, an asset had a redundant companion but that companion has since failed, the remaining asset now has no redundancy and may need to be promoted in its priority.

Third, the assessment review council will conduct a second review of all projects for reasonableness with regard to the replacement value and cost of the project. If there are objections to a project estimated cost, the new recommended project cost should be noted and discussed. If agreed upon, it will be added to the asset record and evaluated to determine if it is appropriate to amend all similar assets within its classification with the new current replacement value.

All modifications to the data and asset recommendations ought to be noted and updated in the database. Following the update, the new assessment reports will be circulated by the database administrator to all members of the assessment review council and the invited stakeholders.

Chapter 9: Reporting, Delivery, and Database Administration

"This analysis and benchmarking to the trustees has built credibility and integrity with the trustees... They understand better what reserves they need in order to meet the long-term needs of their equipment and facilities."[9]
~Douglas K. Christensen

As the assessment review commences, it is important to refer to those items that were discussed and established during the setup phases of the initiative. It is during this effort that many of those initial philosophies will be put to the test and challenged. One key element to revisit and reiterate with the council are the Program Guiding Principles.

In the Guiding Principles, established by the BYU CNA Center and listed in Chapter 4, Principle 5 indicates, "Until there is unity, no action is taken." It worked for BYU but this philosophy may or may not be possible in every organization. Either way, during the assessment review, disagreements in the approach to a specific priority, cost, funding vehicle, or other factor will inevitably arise. When this happens, the Guiding Principles will help to provide clear direction on what the overarching objectives should be and help guide the discussion to a decision point.

Continuing on with the maturation of data, the process is about to enter the understanding and wisdom phases of the Data Refinement Model.[10] The inspection supervisor and inspector have taken the information and validated it into a knowledge base that is more usable to make informed decisions (see Figure 9.1). To understand the data that was gathered during the Zero Tour, a review of the organized information and validated knowledge must be completed by the decision makers. It is now incumbent upon them to apply that knowledge, considering the experience of the inspector, inspection supervisor, as well as their own, to begin to understand what the data is telling them.

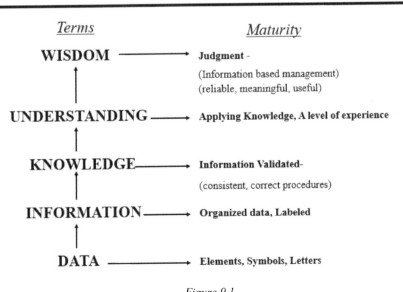

Figure 9.1
Data Refinement Model

Annual Capital Needs Funding

Prioritization of Projects

Once the list of recommended asset renewals, retrofits, and replacements is prepared, the next step is to review and prioritize. It is time to put the prioritization strategy developed during the setup phase to the test. It is at this point where the strategic elements of the program are first challenged. Decisions may be petitioned for, regardless of priority. Some are granted as favors or because of political pressures and it is important to avoid those decisions to maintain the strategic integrity of the program.

During the setup phase, prioritization categories were developed based on the organization's mission and how those needs support fulfilling that mission. Only the assets noted for renewal, retrofit, or replacement will be discussed during the review meetings and senior management presentation. It will be easy for reviewers of the information to be swayed by the limited sampling of the capital needs managed assets. Reminders about the priorities and discussions about the bigger picture will be important components to these deliberations.

As discussions of project priority commence, it is likely that assets will reside in similar classifications and appear to have the identical priority level. That is understandable and unavoidable. It is the duty of the assessment review council to discuss, among other things, the prioritization of the work that is being recommended for action. Consider the Guiding Principles and ensure that the mission comes first. Apply the knowledge and experiences of the council in order to achieve the wisest decision possible.

Funding Request

Until this point in the annual condition assessment, no discussion of funding decisions has taken place. The condition assessments and evaluation of the inspectors' recommendations have been blind to the available funding. In 2004, Doug Christensen wrote, "The purpose is to get a first-hand review of what is really needed to complete a project... Being needs driven has provided [BYU] with the ability to prioritize the need rather than the cost."[11] Now that the assets have been evaluated and the priorities have been established, a discussion regarding the available funding can commence.

Each organization's available funding and funding vehicles are different. Some organizations are able to set aside funds for future use while others are not. Some organizations need to petition the state for capital projects, and those processes may take years to come to fruition before a project is implemented. Some organizations have large endowments that they can tap, while others may be able to issue bonds for their projects. Whatever the opportunities available, it is important to incorporate all of them into the strategic planning as well as an element of which vehicle is the most appropriate.

During the initial inventory and projections laid out in Chapter 5, the estimated annual funding was projected. In the BYU annual needs projection in Figure 5.2, the asset projection indicated funding needs as high as $65 million or as low as $20 million in any given year. However, by funding $31 million into an annual capital needs account, effective management of that fund would ensure the availability of the funds during the highest peaks. If done right, difficult questions of which critical asset not to fund can potentially be avoided.

Clearly, the ideal scenario would be one where the funding, as illustrated in Figure 5.2, is consistently available to meet the needs of the organization. However, understanding that this is not always the case, it is all the more important for the program chief administrator to have a clear understanding of all funding vehicles and which ones are the most appropriate for use. During the review of asset recommendations, available funding should be paired up with the appropriate needs in priority order. For those priorities that do not have readily available funding vehicles, formal requests will need to be submitted. Utilizing the assessment data and asset history compiled and already reported, should provide strong justification for the project needs and objectives.

Executive Reporting
Reporting to the executive team may occur before or after the funding discussions. That depends on the individual organization's funding process and what works best to position resources to support the program. Executive reporting is an important part of the process. It provides transparency with how the funds are being applied and helps to justify continued support of the program. Regardless of when it happens, the team should be sufficiently prepared to present the findings as a recommended plan of action and not just a reiteration of the findings in the report. Without the recommendations from the administrative review council and without the familiarity of the program guiding principles, the prioritization and mission-driven nature of the program may be swayed by subjective qualifiers, and subordinate priority needs may be elevated.

Every executive team is different and will want diverse report formats. Some gravitate toward charts and graphs while others prefer raw financial data and tabular reports. Some prefer to know the details and favor a longer report while others just want the highlights. It is essential to tailor the reporting structure to the desires of the executive team. As mentioned in Chapter 3, it takes knowing the audience in order to have the greatest impact on the message being sent.

The most critical aspect is that it is done in a presentation setting. For BYU, that meant presenting to university administrators as well as the president and board of trustees, who are leaders of the Church of Jesus Christ of Latter-day Saints. This was of such importance that the senior-most leaders of a world-wide church found time to hear about the activities of the CNA Center. With frequent meetings garnering support and buy-in, when challenging financial questions arise, executives will already have an open dialog and can discuss funding strategies rather than blindly cutting capital spending.

Project Delivery
Design and Construction
For those projects that are funded, the effort then shifts to the design and construction team. Sometimes, these are separate groups within the organization; sometimes they are not. Occasionally outside contractors or construction managers execute the project plan. Whatever the relationship, it is vital that the design and construction team have a clear understanding of the objectives of this work.

In an effort to make projects more efficient, assets of a similar type should be grouped together into one project. For example, if there are several places throughout the campus that require carpet replacements, contracting one job for all the replacements could provide a more streamlined project process reducing the overall cost and administrative burden.

An important bridge between the asset management program and the design and construction team is the maintenance and operations team. They work with these assets maintaining and repairing them daily. The maintenance and operations team have the greatest history and information as to what works best and what does not. Too many times, the design and construction team finishes a project and the first time the maintenance and operations team review the scope and work is during commissioning or, worse yet, turnover. More than once, the following exchange has taken place after the project has been completed:

> Technician: "How do I change that?"
> Designer: "It's ok. You won't need to change that for 20 years."
> Technician: "Ok… In 20 years, how will I change that?"

Elements such as asset selection, design review, construction site visits, and allowing the shops to be involved in the entirety of the process will provide a much more functional outcome. Making that effort will also have an overall impact on lowering the total cost of ownership of the asset as well as ensuring a longer life-cycle. In short, the maintenance and operations team should be integrated into the design and construction process from the initial programming.

Database Administration

There is an old saying in the shops: "The job isn't done until the paperwork is submitted." This is no less true during the asset management process. Now that the new asset has been installed, it is vitally important that the data analyst and database administrator are provided the information pertaining to the new asset. Those data elements were all identified during the setup phase of the effort and should be readily available in the standards document that was created at the time. With that data, the database is updated to ensure that this new asset is involved in planning for the future.

Inflation and Market Conditions

Initially, the asset data was inventoried and recorded with current replacement values in today's dollars. Projections were also made in today's dollars. That is the recommended best practice because it provides greater context as to the true needs of the future asset replacements. However, the database will require regular adjustment for inflation and market conditions.

The nuts and bolts of how this happens in the database will vary from one system to another. The important point is that the means of calculating the inflationary percentage is standardized and documented in the standard operating procedures manual for the program. Whether that is the Bureau of Labor Statistics, Consumer Price Index, or some other index, ensuring that it is the same from year to year will help the database remain consistent throughout the years.

Preparing for the Next Zero Tour
Throughout the year, it is important that the capital needs data be managed. During that time, history is being built from preventive maintenance, repairs, downtime, energy consumption, parts, and labor details; all are contributing factors to an effective annual Zero Tour condition assessment when the time comes.

Before the inspection supervisors ever get their list of assets for inspection, the database administrator is working to maintain the data and ensure that histories are being received and audits are being completed. From time to time, construction and renovation projects may be completed outside the asset management process, and the assets as well as the locations will need to be added, deleted, or otherwise updated in the database.

Administrative Review
In order to ensure the database remains accurate, administrative reviewers are to audit data elements annually. To complete a verification of the database, the following steps should be followed:

1. List all items that are missing from the database. This is best completed by reviewing the classification codes summarized within each building and comparing that data juxtaposed with any work that was completed.
2. Verify items that exist in the database. It is best to audit 30% of the assets within each classification of the database annually. Minimum items to audit include:
   - Classification Code
   - Installation Year
   - Life-Cycle
   - Unit Quantity
   - Unit of Measure
   - Unit Cost
   - Location Identification
   In the event an asset audit within a classification codes of a building have an accuracy rate of less than 90%, all assets within the classification code for the building should be audited.
3. Verify the remaining life of all assets with five years of remaining life or less. These assets are not inspected for decision making; they are inspected for reasonableness. If it is reasonable that the asset could continue to perform for the next five years, or whatever the remaining life is estimated, then the remaining life is considered verified. If not, the administrative reviewer would then recommend the life-cycle be adjusted higher or lower accordingly.
4. The administrative reviewer will submit a report of their findings to the program chief administrator for consideration and implementation.

Reoccurring Activities
In addition to continual data verification and management, it is important to keep in mind and continually strategize for the tasks that are required throughout the year to maintain the

program. Table 9.1 provides suggested allocations of tasks for maintaining the asset management program throughout the year. This table will vary from operation to operation, but it is recommended to have something similar in the standard operating procedures handbook for the program.

Task	Program Chief Administrator	Administrative Reviewer	Project Manager	Database Administrator	Data Analyst	Inspection Supervisor(s)	Inspector(s)	Capital Needs Stakeholders	Executive Team
Maintaining Asset Records throughout the Year	✓	✓	✓	✓	✓	✓	✓		
Administrative Review	✓	✓							
Zero Tour Asset Lists				✓	✓				
Organize Inspections for Zero Tour						✓			
Zero Tour Condition Assessment							✓		
Recommendations and Documentation Compiled							✓		
Review of Recommendations						✓	✓		
Senior Review of Recommendations	✓	✓							
Administrative Review Council	✓	✓		✓		✓	✓	✓	
Database Updated with Feedback from Council				✓	✓				
Final Executive Report is Developed	✓	✓		✓					
Annual Capital Needs Executive Presentation	✓							✓	✓
Project Funding Allocated	✓								✓
Project Delivery			✓						
Database Updated with New Asset Data			✓	✓	✓				
Database Upgrades and Backups as Needed				✓	✓				
Database Audit		✓		✓					
Inflation and Market Adjustments	✓	✓	✓	✓	✓	✓	✓		
Standard Operation Procedures Manual Updated		✓		✓	✓	✓	✓		
Periodic Training of Asset Management Program	✓	✓	✓	✓	✓	✓	✓		

Table 9.1

On the surface, the capital needs planning process seems to be an annual occurrence. That couldn't be further from the truth. True capital needs analysis is a constant effort taking into consideration a multitude of data points that are fed into the database every day throughout the operation. Attempting to gather that data as part of the annual exercise will lead to approximations, omissions, and other misinformation that will provide an unsure foundation of data to feed information, knowledge, understanding, and wisdom. By continually maintaining the quality of the data integrity, the capital needs analysis program will have the foundation it needs to ensure the administrators will have the tools needed to make wise investment decisions with their built environment stewardships.

Notes to Part III

[1] Ibid.

[2] Ibid.

[3] Christensen, "Professional Leadership and the Strategic Assessment Model."

[4] Christensen, "Standing on Shoulders."

[5] Christensen, "Capital Needs Analysis."

[6] Christensen, "Recapitalization Management."

[7] Ibid.

[8] Ibid.

[9] Christensen, "Capital Needs Analysis."

[10] Rose et al., *Buildings…The Gifts That Keep on Taking*.

[11] Rose, *Charting a New Course for Campus Renewal*.

Part IV: Wrap Up

Chapter 10: The Learning Organization

"Our collective ability to assess where we are in relation to things that matter and, more important, to see where we need to be going in the future and ensure that we have the leadership ability to get to that vision will be critical to our success."
~ Douglas K. Christensen

Enterprise asset management through a capital needs analysis program such as this can appear complex, but in reality, the concepts are quite simple. There are several interwoven threads throughout this process that must be maintained in order to be successful (see Figure 10.1).

Total Cost of Ownership

The total cost of ownership model is the concept that pulls it all together (see Figure 10.1).[1] Only by maintaining a clear perspective of all elements of the TCO model can effective asset management planning happen. Without considering project delivery, operations and maintenance, or utilities when planning for recapitalization projects, they will be limited in their ability to maximize return on investment. Only by breaking down those silos can true TCO be achieved.

Figure 10.1
Asset Life-cycle Model for
Total Cost of Ownership Management

Leadership and Change

Incorporating any change initiative takes leadership. Leadership means having the courage to do the right thing.[2] Without an appropriate sense of urgency and a team to sponsor the process, the asset management program will flounder rather than be an integrated piece of the organization's key strategy for success. By maintaining the vision of what it can be, collaborating on the strategy, and persevering through the obstacles, true leaders can work to ensure that this change strategy is robust enough to survive (see Figure 10.2).

Figure 10.2
Strategic Balanced Demands

Data-Driven Decision Making

Any successful enterprise asset management process will have a strong foundation of accurate data, but that data will only go so far. By using the data to inform the decision-making process, that knowledge can lead to understanding and wisdom. Data such as life-cycle, cost of maintenance, utility consumption, and other

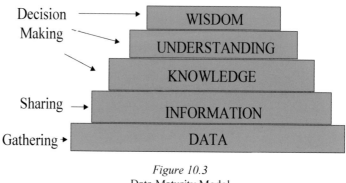

Figure 10.3
Data Maturity Model

raw data factors, when analyzed, can drive wise decisions that will provide greater return on the asset investment (see Figure 10.3).[3]

Mission-Driven Strategy

As Doug Christensen stated in his introduction, "The profession of Facilities Management has continually shifted every moment and different drivers of change have had their influence on it." Having a rigid program, being unyielding in the means and methods, or failing to adapt standards to the changing environment will inevitably leave the asset management program by the wayside. This is only understood by maintaining communication with stakeholders and senior leaders of the organization. Some organizations change and evolve faster than others. Regardless of the rate of change, the asset management process must rise to meet the challenge.

Figure 10.4
Enterprise Asset Management

Visionary Priorities

Throughout the years of administering this program, priorities will be challenged. Priorities must be established and adapted to support the mission of the organization. When challenged, having the established priority on the mission and vision of the future of the organization, the program's primary objectives will endure.

Bottom-Up Assessments

Countless facility condition assessments have been conducted with only senior leadership being involved in the process. With the exception of being the occasional guide, the front-line technicians who work with the assets day in and day out are not involved in the process until after the assessment is completed and reports are being distributed. Involving the technicians who have intimate knowledge of the function and history of the assets is critical in developing a holistic perspective of the asset and which strategies should be employed to maximize the return on investment.

Assessment and Continuous Improvement

As the old saying goes, "In order to know where you are going, you have to know where you have been." As a part of each annual review and assessment, the participants of the asset management program should compile their lessons learned for the year and incorporate them into the program standards. The built environment is ever-changing, and with the advent of technological evolution, that rate of change increases exponentially. Remaining static with an attitude of "That's the way we have always done it" will doom the program in short order. "Assessment is not an end in and of itself, but rather a strategic tool for continuous improvement."[4]

Collaboration

From the initial development of the foundational elements of the program through the Zero Tours and executive presentations, the asset management program thrives on collaboration. Without it, the program elements, priorities, and guiding principles go unsupported and the program fails. Priorities that only meet the needs of the facilities organization with no consideration for the mission of the organization will be seen as self-serving. A collaborative effort throughout must be maintained.

Learning Organization

As stated in the APPA Body of Knowledge, "Recapitalization is the learning organization of facilities managers."[5] It is in the midst of the capital needs analysis process and evaluating asset performance for future mission-driven decision making, we have the ability to initiate course corrections and ensure that the next generation of assets experiences more of a return on investment. Taking full advantage of these opportunities to conduct a thorough assessment of how business is being managed and assets are performing will be key to success in every facet of the facilities organization.

There is more to learn as we continue to progress on how to better manage the existing built environments. As the role of total cost of ownership is better understood and applied, the growth of BIM and the movement toward life-cycle management will give the profession new direction. Recapitalization management, using life-cycle and total cost of ownership principles, is a platform for change.[6]

Notes to Part IV

[1] Christensen, "Recapitalization Management."
[2] Bennis, *On Becoming a Leader*.
[3] Christensen, "What Is TCO? Why TCO?"
[4] Cain and Christensen, "Assessment and Continuous Improvement."
[5] Christensen, "Recapitalization Management."
[6] Ibid.

Summary of Figures and Tables

Figure i.1, 8.1, & 10.3: The Data Maturity Model

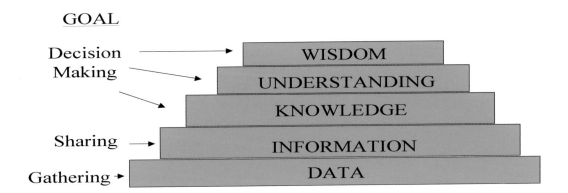

Figure 1.1: TCO Management Silos

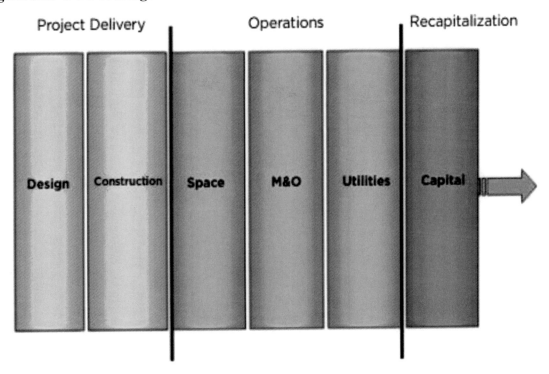

Figure 1.2 & 10.1: Asset Life-cycle Model for Total Cost of Ownership Management

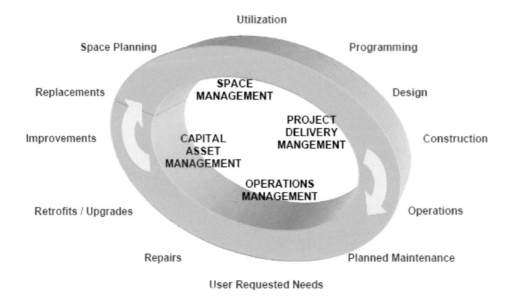

Figure 1.3: Total Cost of Ownership Framework

Birth & Burial (non-recurring)

Cost A	Concept to Bid
Cost B	Financing
Cost C	Construction/ Install
Cost K	Decommission/Demolition/Disposal

Maintenance & Operations (annual recurring)

Cost D	Operations
Cost E	Planned Maintenance/Routine
Cost F	Repairs/Breakdowns
Cost G	Utilities

Recapitalization (periodic recurring)

Cost H	Retrofits/Improvements
Cost I	Programmatic Upgrade
Cost J	Replacement/Renewal

Figure 1.4: Strategic Investment Pyramid

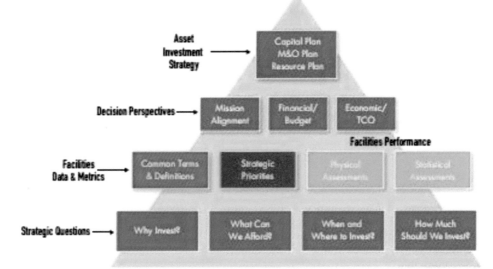

INTEGRATED DECISION FRAMEWORK

Figure 1.5: Asset Comprehensive Plan

Total Cost of Ownership
"Asset Investment Strategy"

Capital Needs Plan

- Retrofit Project
- Improvement Projects
- Mandatory/Compliance Projects
- Capital Renewal/Repalcements
- Life Cycle Plan

Operations Plan

- Work Hours/Human Power Needs
- Materials/Supllies Needs
- Equipment/Tools Needs
- Systems/Process Needs
- Energy & Utilities Plan

Growth & Impact Plan

- Additions
- Additional Buildings/Facilities
- Expand Infrastructure
- Space Plan
- Property Expansion

Figure 2.1 & 10.2: Strategic Balanced Demands

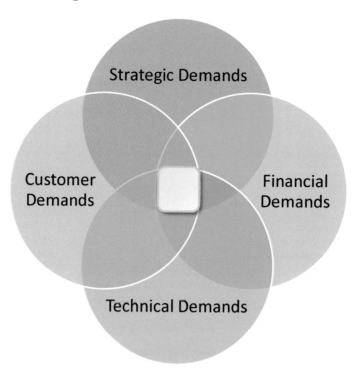

Strategic Demands

Customer Demands

Financial Demands

Technical Demands

Table 3.1: Possible Opportunities and Impacts of Planned vs. Emergency Replacements

Table 3.1		
	Possible Opportunities Associated with Planned Replacement	**Possible Impacts Associated with Emergency Replacement**
Asset Failure	Delivery before failure and loss of business	Unexpected loss of business or occupancy Create a hazardous condition
Mission Fit	Ability to analyze the asset mission fit and future plans	A type-for-type replacement regardless of needs or future planning
Planning & Analytics	Engineering of replacement asset based on current and future needs	Rushed engineering and analytics if completed
Evaluation of Options	Evaluation of various options and comparison of total cost of ownership impact	Comparison of total cost of ownership likely omitted in the name of expedience
Bidding & Procurement	Bid process ensuring a competitive price	Abbreviated bidding process compromising competition
Project Delivery	Strategic project delivery allowing for the most cost effective and least disruptive means and methods	Rushed shipping and fabrication costs Expedited project delivery requiring rework Greater likelihood of unforeseeable conditions

Table 4.1: Seven Basic Assessment Levels

Assessment Level	Definition	Method	Results	Decision Making	Long-Term Plan	Business Fit
No Assessment	No awareness of asset status	None	Emergencies and surprises	Crisis-driven	None	Assets not planned properly
Breakdown Assessment	Wait until asset fails before assessing needs	Communicate failures as they happen	Emergencies and surprises	As needed, at the time	None	Resources not planned properly
Parametric Assessment	Statistical analysis of asset resource needs without inventory details	Detail sample gathering and extrapolating sample results over remaining assets	Global projection of resource needs without specific details	Determines potential investment need	Snapshot of needs based on statistical sampling	Large complex areas that need to know how big the problem is' not fit for managing
General Condition Assessment	A snapshot review of current asset conditions focused on projects needed at the time of assessment.	Visual look at the condition of assets with project scope and cost estimates	A list of projects and priorities that need to be completed	Complete projects identified in the assessment; unplanned failures would be a surprise	Snapshot of needs; typically only projected every 3 to 5 years as needed and as resources become available	Places where a current scope of work, priorities, and cost estimates are needed to improve current assets; little future consideration with assets excluded from assessment
Detailed Condition Assessment	A snapshot review of asset conditions and projections of needs for 3 to 5 years at the time of the assessment	A greater detail review of asset needs, scope, and cost estimates	List of projects and priorities that need to be completed	Complete projects identified in the assessment; unplanned failures would be a surprise	Snapshot of needs; typically only projected every 3 to 5 years as needed and as resources become available	Places where a current scope of work, priorities, and cost estimates are needed to improve current assets; little future consideration with assets excluded from assessment
Life-cycle Assessment	Detailed inventory of assets where life-cycle is tracked and decisions are made on life-cycle	Inventory of all assets, systems, and components; determine remaining life-cycle, set replacement costs, and manage assets according to remaining life-cycle	Annual inspection of all assets, systems, and components where the remaining life-cycle at or below 1 or 2 years remaining determining which need to be refurbished, retrofit, replaced, or are to continue in their current state	Matches high priority assets requiring replacement with limited resource availability weighing the impact of inaction	Inventory allows for long-range projection of asset needs for the life-cycle of all assets managed by the program	Places where projecting the need and level of resources, inspecting current needs, and setting priorities are needed to make good long-term decisions
Lifetime Assessment	Detailed inventory of assets where all costs are tracked and useful life decisions are made	Inventory all assets, systems, and components, set life-cycle and replacement costs, manage remaining life, and track all costs related to the assets	Annual inspection of all assets, systems, and components where the remaining life-cycle is at or below 1 or 2 years determining which assets are to be refurbished, retrofit, replaced, or are to continue in their current state	Matches high priority assets requiring replacement with limited resource availability weighing the impact of inaction while also considering the actual realized cost of maintaining the asset	The inventory and cost tracking allows for projecting the resource and asset needs for the life-cycle of all assets being managed	Places where projecting the needs and level of resources, inspecting current needs, setting high priority needs, and tracking all costs related to assets is needed to make good long-term decisions

Figure 5.1: Levels of Assets

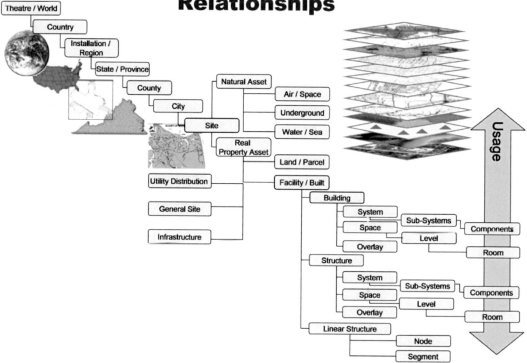

Figure 5.2: BYU CNA Center 40-year Trend

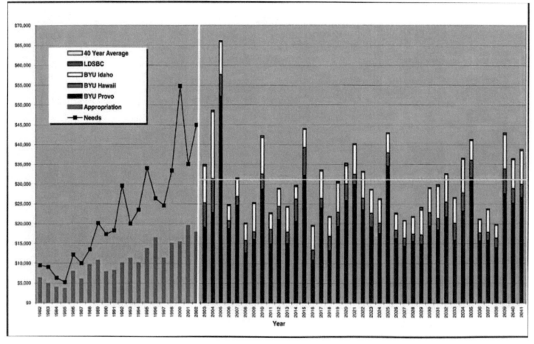

Figure 6.1: Effective Quality Assurance

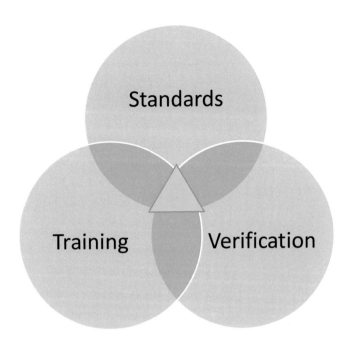

Table 7.1: Evaluation Factors to Consider

General Items…	For Architectural Elements…	For Dynamic Equipment…
✓ Safety Concerns ✓ Functionality ✓ Performing as Designed ✓ Meeting the Intended Use ✓ Meeting the Current Needs ✓ Visual Inspection of General Condition ✓ Remaining Warranty	✓ Stains or Wear Patterns ✓ Separated Seams or Rippling ✓ Missing Grout ✓ Outdated Aesthetically ✓ Tiles Broken or Missing ✓ Missing or Cracked Veneer ✓ Standing Water on Roofs ✓ Drains in Good Repair ✓ Unwanted Vegetation ✓ Functioning Windows ✓ Thermal Intrusion ✓ Moisture Intrusion	✓ General Function ✓ Vibration Analysis ✓ Thermal Imaging ✓ Energy Consumption ✓ Piping and Valves ✓ Safety Devices ✓ Cabling and Insulation ✓ Failed Components ✓ Availability of Replacement Parts ✓ Refrigerant Type

Figure 8.2 & 9.1: Data Refinement Model

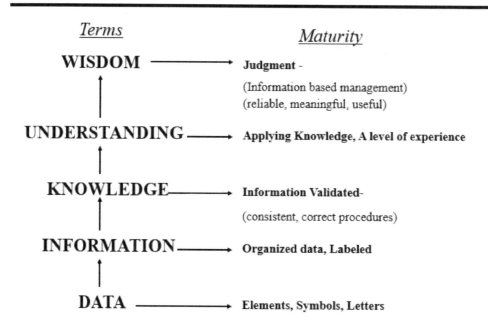

Data Refinement Model

Terms	Maturity
WISDOM →	Judgment - (Information based management) (reliable, meaningful, useful)
↑	
UNDERSTANDING →	Applying Knowledge, A level of experience
↑	
KNOWLEDGE →	Information Validated- (consistent, correct procedures)
↑	
INFORMATION →	Organized data, Labeled
↑	
DATA →	Elements, Symbols, Letters

Table 9.1: Table of Program Activities

Task	Program Chief Administrator	Administrative Reviewer	Project Manager	Database Administrator	Data Analyst	Inspection Supervisor(s)	Inspector(s)	Capital Needs Stakeholders	Executive Team
Maintaining Asset Records throughout the Year	✓	✓	✓	✓	✓	✓	✓		
Administrative Review	✓	✓							
Zero Tour Asset Lists				✓	✓				
Organize Inspections for Zero Tour						✓			
Zero Tour Condition Assessment							✓		
Recommendations and Documentation Compiled							✓		
Review of Recommendations						✓	✓		
Senior Review of Recommendations	✓	✓							
Administrative Review Council	✓	✓		✓		✓	✓	✓	
Database Updated with Feedback from Council				✓	✓				
Final Executive Report is Developed	✓	✓		✓					
Annual Capital Needs Executive Presentation	✓							✓	✓
Project Funding Allocated	✓								✓
Project Delivery			✓						
Database Updated with New Asset Data			✓	✓	✓				
Database Upgrades and Backups as Needed			✓	✓					
Database Audit		✓		✓					
Inflation and Market Adjustments	✓	✓	✓	✓	✓	✓	✓		
Standard Operation Procedures Manual Updated		✓		✓	✓	✓	✓		
Periodic Training of Asset Management Program	✓	✓	✓	✓	✓	✓	✓		

Table 9.1

Figure 10.4: Enterprise Asset Management

Additional resources can be found at
www.BuildingTEAMSBook.com

Bibliography

Bennis, Warren. *On Becoming a Leader*. Philadelphia, PA: Basic Books, 2003.

Cain, David, and Douglas K Christensen. "Assessment and Continuous Improvement." *Facilities Manager*, no. January/February (2000): 19–20.

Christensen, Douglas K. "A Study of Decision Criteria for Major Replacements, Renewals, and Planned Improvements at Selected University Campuses." Brigham Young University, 1984.

———. "Capital Needs Analysis." *Facilities Manager*, no. September/October (2004): 49–51.

———. "Capital Needs Analysis Principles," 1981.

———. "Integrating Capital Studies within Physical Plant Operations." *Facilities Manager*, no. Fall (1986): 20–25. https://www.appa.org/membershipawards/documents/1987.pdf.

———. "Professional Leadership and the Strategic Assessment Model." In *SAM: The Strategic Assessment Model*, edited by Jayne Sutton and EEI Communications, 2nd ed., 17–26. Alexandria, VA: APPA, 2001.

———. "Recapitalization Management." *APPA Body of Knowledge*, 2011. http://bokcms.appa.org/subchapter_view.cfm?chap_id=92&part_id=2.

———. "Standing on Shoulders." *Facilities Manager*, no. November/December (2009): 14–15.

———. "What Is TCO? Why TCO?" *Facilities Manager*, no. July/August (2016): 21–23.

Christensen, Douglas K., Rodney Rose, and Terry Ruprecht. "A Common Vocabulary for Asset Investment Strategy." *Facilities Manager*, no. March/April (2007): 26–30.

Dana K. Smith, FAIA, DKS Information Consulting, LLC: Used with Permission

Davenport, Thomas H. "Competing on Analytics." *Harvard Business Review*, January (2006).

Leroy, Wayne E., E. Lander Medlin, and Steve Glazner. "Vision, People, and Process: An Interview with APPA President Doug Christensen." *Facilities Manager*, Fall (1995): 14–23.

"Luke 14:28." In *KJV Bible*, n.d.

Rose, Rodney. *Charting a New Course for Campus Renewal*. Alexandria, VA, 1999.

Rose, Rodney, David Cain, James Dempsey, and Rich Schneider. *Buildings... The Gifts That Keep on Taking*. Alexandria, VA: APPA, 2007.

Taylor, John. "The Organization of the Church." *The Millennial Star* 13, no. 22 (1851): 339.

The Doctrine and Covenants. Salt Lake City, UT, USA: The Church of Jesus Christ of Latter-day Saints, 2013.

Made in the USA
Lexington, KY
29 July 2018